JEFFERSON'S LEGACY

A Brief History of the Library of Congress

JEFFERSON'S LEGACY

A Brief History of the Library of Congress

John Y. Cole

LIBRARY OF CONGRESS · WASHINGTON · 1993

THIS PUBLICATION WAS MADE POSSIBLE BY GENEROUS SUPPORT FROM THE JAMES MADISON COUNCIL, A NATIONAL, PRIVATE-SECTOR ADVISORY COUNCIL DEDICATED TO HELPING THE LIBRARY OF CONGRESS SHARE ITS UNIQUE RESOURCES WITH THE NATION AND THE WORLD.

John Y. Cole, a librarian and historian, began working at the Library of Congress in 1966. He has been director of the Center for the Book in the Library of Congress since it was established in 1977. The author wishes to acknowledge the assistance of Margaret E. Wagner of the Library's Publishing Office in the preparation of this volume, which is dedicated to the memory of David C. Mearns, who served the Library from 1918 until he retired in 1967.

LIBRARY OF CONGRESS CATALOGING-IN-PUBLICATION DATA

Cole, John Young, 1940–
     Jefferson's legacy : a brief history of the Library of Congress / by John Y. Cole.
       p.   cm.
     Includes bibliographical references.
     ISBN 0-8444-0764-X
     ——— ——— Z663 .J44 1993
     1. Library of Congress — History. 2. National libraries — United States — History.
I. Title.
     Z733.U6C567 1993   92-30311
     027.573 — dc20   CIP

Cover photograph and photos on pages 6, 10, 30, 33, 34, 49, 58, 76–77, 78, 83, 86, 87, and 89 by Reid Baker. Photos pages 8–9 and page 90 by Jim Higgins. Photo page 82 by Marita Clance.

Book design by Robert L. Wiser, Meadows & Wiser, Washington, D.C.

For sale by the U.S. Government Printing Office
Superintendent of Documents, Mail Stop: SSOP, Washington, D.C. 20402-9328
ISBN 0-16-041653-1

Contents

Preface

The Library of Congress, America's oldest national cultural institution, will be two hundred years old in the year 2000. With generous support from the U.S. Congress, it has become the largest repository of recorded knowledge in the world and a symbol of the vital connection between knowledge and democracy.

Thomas Jefferson's Library, the seed from which today's Library of Congress grew, is now housed in the Rare Book and Special Collections Division. The volume in the foreground is a work by sixteenth-century master architect Andrea Palladio, whose classical influence can be seen in Jefferson's own architectural designs.

If ever a library had a single founder, Thomas Jefferson is the founder of the Library of Congress. His personal library is the Library's core, and the vast range of his interests determined the universal and diverse nature of the Library's collections and activities. The active mind was central to Jefferson's concept of government; he felt there was "no subject to which a Member of Congress may not have occasion to refer." He believed that self-government depended on the free, unhampered pursuit of truth by an informed and involved citizenry. Today's Library of Congress epitomizes Jefferson's faith in learning and his practical determination to make democracy work.

In this bicentennial decade, the Library of Congress will honor its founder and renew its commitment to the knowledge-based society that Jefferson envisioned. The Library not only provides information and ideas to Congress and the nation; it also sets cataloging and bibliographic standards that are used by libraries throughout the world. It is testing new electronic technologies that will share the Library's collections with schools and research institutions across America and, ultimately, with all the people of America and the world. Today it also is helping parliamentary libraries in emerging democracies of Eastern Europe and the former Soviet Union become effective resources and catalysts of change. When the renovation and restoration work in the Library's Thomas Jefferson Building is completed in the mid-1990s, this magnificent structure will contain reading rooms representing the cultural legacies of the entire world.

The unleashed, unlimited pursuit of truth may be the last frontier and the ultimate proving ground for our American ideal of freedom. In a world of increasing physical restraints and limitations, it is only in the life of the mind and spirit that the horizons of freedom can remain truly infinite. We must rediscover what we should have known all along, that the pursuit of truth is the noblest part of Jefferson's legacy.

James H. Billington
The Librarian of Congress

The Library of Congress, 1800–1992

A researcher stands under the dome of the Main Reading Room of the first Library of Congress building, now named for Thomas Jefferson.

The Library of Congress occupies a unique place in American civilization. Established as a legislative library in 1800, it grew into a national institution in the nineteenth century. Since World War II, it has become an international resource of unparalleled dimensions.

In 1950, the sesquicentennial year of the Library of Congress, the eminent librarian S. R. Ranganathan paid the Library and the U.S. Congress an unusual tribute:

The institution serving as the national library of the United States is perhaps more fortunate than its predecessors in other countries. It has the Congress as its godfather ... This stroke of good fortune has made it perhaps the most influential of all the national libraries of the world.[1]

Forty-two years later, the Library built by the U.S. Congress has achieved an even greater degree of prominence. Since 1950 the size of its collections and staff have tripled, and its annual appropriation has soared from $9 million to more than $330 million. With collections totaling more than 100 million items, a staff of nearly 5,000 persons, and services unmatched in scope by any other research library, the Library of Congress is one of the world's leading cultural institutions.[2]

The diversity of the Library of Congress is startling. Simultaneously it serves as: a legislative library and the major research arm of the U.S. Congress; the copyright agency of the United States; a center for scholarship that collects research materials in many media and in most subjects from throughout the world in more than 450 languages; a public institution that is open to everyone over high school age and serves readers in twenty-two reading rooms; a government library that is heavily used by the executive branch and the judiciary; a national library for the blind and physically handicapped; an outstanding law library; one of the world's largest providers of bibliographic data and products; a center for the commissioning and performance of chamber music; the home of the nation's poet laureate; the sponsor of exhibitions and of musical, literary, and cultural programs that reach across the nation and the world; a research center for the preservation and conservation of library materials; and the world's largest repository of maps, atlases, printed and recorded music, motion pictures, and television programs.

The Library of Congress occupies three massive structures on Capitol Hill, near the U.S. Capitol. The Jefferson Building, opened in 1897, is a grand monument to civilization, culture, and American achievement. The functional Adams Building was opened in 1939. The modern Madison Building, completed in 1980, is by far the largest structure. About two million researchers, scholars, and tourists visit the Library of Congress each year and millions more use its services.

Since its creation, the Library of Congress has been part of the legislative branch of the American government, and even though it is recognized as the de facto national library of the United States, it does not have that official designation. Nevertheless, it performs those functions performed by national libraries elsewhere and has become a symbol of American democracy and faith in the power of learning.

How did a library established by the legislature for its own use become such an ambitious, multipurpose institution? Two points are clear: the expansion of the Library's functions derives from the expansion of its collections; and the growth of the institution is tied to the growth and ambitions of the entire American nation. The development of the Library of Congress cannot be separated from the history of the nation it serves. Nor can it be separated from the philosophy and ideals of Thomas Jefferson, its principal founder.

The Library of Congress was established as the fledgling legislature of the new Republic prepared to move from Philadelphia to the new capital city of Washington. On April 24, 1800, Pres. John Adams approved legislation that appropriated $5,000 to purchase "such books as may be necessary for the use of Congress." The first books, ordered from London, arrived in 1801 and were stored in the U.S. Capitol, the Library's first home. The collection consisted of 740 volumes and three maps.

On January 26, 1802, Pres. Thomas Jefferson approved the first law defining the role and functions of the new institution. This measure created the post of Librarian of Congress and gave Congress, through a Joint Committee on the Library, the authority to establish the Library's budget and its rules and regulations. From the beginning, however, the institution was more than just a legislative library, for the 1802 law made the appointment of the Librarian of Congress a presidential responsibility. It also permitted the president and vice president to borrow books, a privilege that, in the next three decades, was extended to most government agencies and to the judiciary. A separate law department was approved in 1832, along with an appropriation to purchase law books under the guidance of the chief justice of the United States.

Three developments in the Library's early history permanently established the institution's national roots. First, the Library of Congress was created by the national legislature, which took direct responsibility for its operation. Second, the Library of Congress served as the first library of the American *government*. Finally, in 1815, the scope of the Library's collection was permanently expanded. The ideals, intellectual curiosity, and pragmatism of Thomas Jefferson (1743–1826) were the keys to this transformation.

Jefferson believed that the power of the intellect could shape a free and democratic society. As a man who stated he could not live without books, he took a keen interest in the Library of Congress and its collection while he was president of the United States from 1801 to 1809. Throughout his presidency, he personally recommended books for the Library, and he appointed the first two Librarians of Congress. In 1814, the British army invaded the city of Washington and burned the Capitol, including the 3,000-volume Library of Congress. By then retired to Monticello, Jefferson offered to sell his personal library, the largest and finest in the country, to the Congress to "recommence" its library. The purchase of Jefferson's 6,487 volumes for $23,940 was approved in 1815.

The library that Jefferson sold to Congress not only included over twice the number of volumes that had been in the destroyed Library of Congress, it expanded the scope of the Library far beyond the bounds of a legislative library devoted primarily to legal, economic, and historical works. Jefferson was a man of encyclopedic interests, and his library included works on architecture, the arts, science, literature, and geography. It contained books in French, Spanish, German, Latin, Greek, and one three-volume statistical work in Russian. He believed that the American legislature needed ideas and information on all subjects and in many languages in order to govern a democracy. Anticipating the argument that his collection might be too comprehensive, he argued that there was "no subject to which a Member of Congress may not have occasion to refer."[3]

The acquisition by Congress of Jefferson's library provided the base for the expansion of the Library's functions. The Jeffersonian concept of universality is the rationale for the comprehensive collecting policies of today's Library of Congress. Jefferson's belief in the power of knowledge and the direct link between knowledge and democracy shaped the Library's philosophy of sharing its collections and services as widely as possible.

One congressman who favored the purchase of Jefferson's library expressed a growing cultural nationalism in the United States when he argued that it would make "a most admirable substratum for a National Library." Many Americans, aware of the cultural dependence of the United States on Europe, were anxious that their country establish its own traditions and institutions. For example, an editorial in the July 15, 1815, (Washington, D.C.) daily *National Intelligencer* pointed out: "In all civilized nations of Europe there are national libraries . . . In a country of such general intelligence as this, the Congressional or National Library of the United States [should] become the great repository of the literature of the world."

Yet even as the Library was beginning to grow, it appeared that the Smithsonian Institution might become the American national library. During the early 1850s, the Smithsonian's talented and aggressive librarian, Charles Coffin Jewett, tried to move the institution in that direction and turn it into a national bibliographical center. Jewett's efforts were opposed, however, by Smithsonian secretary Joseph Henry, who insisted that the Smithsonian focus its activities on scientific research and publication. In fact, the secretary favored the eventual development of a national library at the Library of Congress, which he viewed as the appropriate foundation for "a collection of books worthy of a Government whose perpetuity principally depends on the intelligence of the people." On July 10, 1854, Henry dismissed Jewett, ending any possibility that the Smithsonian might become the national library. Moreover, twelve years later, Henry readily agreed to the transfer of the entire forty thousand-volume library of the Smithsonian Institution to the Library of Congress.

The Library of Congress suffered difficult times during the 1850s. The growing intersectional rivalry between North and South hindered the strengthening of any government institution. Furthermore, in late 1851 the most serious fire in the Library's history destroyed about two-thirds of its fifty-five thousand volumes, including two-thirds of Jefferson's library. Congress responded quickly and generously: in 1852 a total of $168,700 was appropriated to restore the Library's rooms in the Capitol and to replace the lost books. But the books were to be replaced only, with no particular intention of supplementing or expanding the collection. This policy reflected the conservative philosophy of Librarian of Congress John Silva Meehan and Sen. James A. Pearce of Maryland, the chairman of the Joint Committee on the Library, who favored keeping a strict limit on the Library's activities.

A few years later the Library lost several collection-building functions, fur-

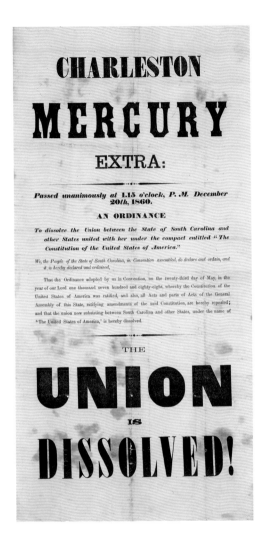

CHARLESTON

MERCURY

EXTRA:

Passed unanimously at 1.15 o'clock, P. M. December
20th, 1860.

AN ORDINANCE

To dissolve the Union between the State of South Carolina and
other States united with her under the compact entitled "The
Constitution of the United States of America."

We, the People of the State of South Carolina, in Convention assembled, do declare and ordain, and
it is hereby declared and ordained,

That the Ordinance adopted by us in Convention, on the twenty-third day of May, in the
year of our Lord one thousand seven hundred and eighty-eight, whereby the Constitution of the
United States of America was ratified, and also, all Acts and parts of Acts of the General
Assembly of this State, ratifying amendments of the said Constitution, are hereby repealed;
and that the union now subsisting between South Carolina and other States, under the name of
"The United States of America," is hereby dissolved.

THE

UNION

IS

DISSOLVED!

This Charleston
Mercury *broadside*
of December 20, 1860,
housed in the Rare
Book and Special
Collections Division, is
but one of many thou-
sands of items in the
Library's unparalleled
Civil War collections.

ther impeding its progress toward the comprehensive collection that Mr. Jefferson had favored. In the 1830s and 1840s, the Library of Congress had begun distributing public documents to institutions throughout the United States and exchanging books and documents with foreign institutions on behalf of the U.S. government. A joint resolution of Congress in 1857 transferred responsibility for public document distribution to the Bureau of Interior and responsibility for international exchange of books and documents to the Department of State. Moreover, in 1859 all U.S. copyright activities were centralized at the Patent Office, which meant that the Library of Congress and the Smithsonian Institution no longer received the copies of books and pamphlets deposited for copyright that had been sent to each institution since 1846.

Two years later, in 1861, newly elected president Abraham Lincoln replaced Librarian Meehan with John G. Stephenson, an Indiana physician. Stephenson served a relatively short term of four years as Librarian. A political appointee, his major concerns were outside the Library. In fact, he was a volunteer aide-de-camp at the battles of Chancellorsville and Gettysburg. As the Civil War came to a close, the Library had a staff of only seven and a collection of only eighty thousand volumes; nonetheless, thanks to the vision and impetus of Thomas Jefferson, its national character was indisputable.

The person responsible for transforming the Library of Congress into an institution of national significance in the Jeffersonian spirit was Ainsworth Rand Spofford, a former Cincinnati bookseller and journalist who served as Librarian of Congress from 1865 until 1897. Spofford accomplished this task by permanently linking the legislative and national functions of the Library, first in practice and then, through the 1897 reorganization of the Library, in law. He provided his successors as Librarian with four essential prerequisites for the development of an American national library: (1) firm, bipartisan congressional support for the notion of the Library of Congress as both a legislative and a national library; (2) the beginning of a comprehensive collection of Americana; (3) a magnificent new building, itself a national monument; and (4) a strong and independent office of Librarian of Congress. It was Spofford who had the interest, skill, and perseverance to capitalize on the Library of Congress's claim

Mathew B. Brady provided an invaluable service to history when he organized a staff of field photographers who compiled an extraordinary pictorial record of the Civil War. Among the portraits of Civil War commanders included in the Library's Brady-Handy Collection in the Prints and Photographs Division are these of the ultimately victorious Ulysses S. Grant, above, who had found a moment to relax with his wife and son, and revered Confederate general Robert E. Lee, at right.

to a national role. Each Librarian of Congress since Spofford has built upon his accomplishments. Each has shaped the institution in a different way, but none has wavered from Jefferson's belief that the democratic form of government depended on a comprehensive base of knowledge and information.

The idea of an American national library that Spofford revived had been languishing since Jewett's departure from the Smithsonian in 1854. Spofford and Jewett shared several ideas relating to a national library; in particular, both recognized the importance of copyright deposit in developing a comprehensive collection of a nation's literature. Yet there was a major difference in their views. Spofford never envisioned the Library of Congress as the center of a network of American libraries, a focal point for providing other libraries with cataloging and bibliographic services. Instead, he viewed it, in the European model, as a unique, independent institution—a single, comprehensive collection of national literature to be used both by Congress and the American people. Congress needed such a collection because, as Spofford paraphrased Jefferson, "there is almost no work, within the vast range of literature and science, which may not at some time prove useful to the legislature of a great nation." It was imperative, he felt, that such a great national collection be shared with all citizens, for the United States was "a Republic which rests upon the popular intelligence."[4]

Immediately after the Civil War, American society began a rapid transformation; one of the major changes was the expansion of the federal government. Spofford took full advantage of the favorable political and cultural climate, and the increasing national confidence, to promote the Library's expansion. He always believed that the Library of Congress *was* the national library and he used every conceivable argument to convince others, particularly the Joint Committee on the Library and their colleagues in the rest of Congress.

In the first years of his administration Spofford obtained congressional approval of six laws or resolutions that ensured a national role for the Library of Congress. The legislative acts were: an appropriation providing for the expansion of the Library in the Capitol building, approved in early 1865; the copyright amendment of 1865, which once again brought copyright deposits into the Library's collections; the Smithsonian deposit of 1866, whereby the entire library of the Smithsonian Institution, a collection especially strong in scientific materials, was transferred to the Library; the 1867 purchase, for $100,000, of the private library of historian and archivist Peter Force, establishing the foundation of the Library's Americana and incunabula collections; the international exchange resolution of 1867, providing for the development of the Library's collection of foreign public documents; and the copyright act of 1870, which brought *all* U.S. copyright registration and deposit activities to the Library.

The centralization of copyright activities at the Library was Spofford's most impressive collection-building feat. The first U.S. copyright law was approved in 1790, but the practice of depositing items registered for copyright protection in libraries for use was not enacted until 1846, when the newly established Smithsonian Institution and the Library of Congress obtained the privilege. The Library of Congress received single copies of deposits from 1846 until 1859 and, thanks to Spofford, the practice started again in 1865. Enforcement was a problem, however, and Spofford decided he needed the authority that would come from centralizing all registration and deposit activities at the Library, consolidating functions then performed at

the Patent Office and by the district courts. The copyright law of 1870 ensured the continuing development of the Library's Americana collections, for it stipulated that two copies of every book, pamphlet, map, print, photograph, and piece of music registered for copyright be deposited in the Library, a requirement that certainly would have met with Jefferson's approval. The international copyright law of 1891, which gave protection to works of foreign origin under certain conditions of reciprocal protection, added further luster to the Library's collections, for it brought deposits of foreign works into the Library for the first time.

In its 1876 survey of the libraries of the United States, the U.S. Bureau of Education listed the rapidly growing Library of Congress and the Boston Public Library as the two largest libraries in the United States, with approximately 300,000 volumes apiece. By 1897, when the Library moved from its overcrowded rooms in the Capitol across the east plaza into its spacious new

By 1890, the need for space in the Library's quarters in the Capitol was desperate—books and mail bags were piled high. The situation was eased considerably when the Library was moved to its own building in 1897.

building, its collections ranked first among American libraries in size and scope. Over 40 percent of its 840,000 volumes and at least 90 percent of its map, music, and graphic arts collections had been acquired through copyright deposit. Important items deposited through copyright included Civil War photographs by Mathew Brady and what are usually considered the first motion pictures.

The copyright privilege not only influenced the development of the Library's collections, it also helped determine the direction of their growth. When the Library of Congress moved into its new building, separate custodial units were established for the special collections formed primarily

ohannes Dei gratia rex Anglie dominus Hybernie dux Normannie et Aquitanie comes Andegavie archiepiscopis episcopis abbatibus comitibus baronibus iusticiarus forestariis vicecomitibus prepositis ministris et omnibus ballivis et fidelibus suis salutem Sciatis nos intuitu Dei et pro salute anime nostre et omnium antecessorum et heredum nostrorum ad honorem Dei et exaltationem sancte ecclesie et emendationem regni nostri per consilium venerabilium patrum nostrorum Stephani Cant' archiepiscopi totius Anglie primatis et sancte Romane ecclesie cardinalis Henrici Dublin' archiepiscopi Willelmi London' Petri Winton' Joscelini Bathon' et Glaston' Hugonis Lincoln' Walteri Wygorn' Willelmi Coventr' et Benedicti Roff' episcoporum magistri Pandulfi domini pape subdiaconi et familiaris et fratris Ermerici magistri milicie templi in Anglia et nobilium virorum Willelmi Mariscalli comitis Penbroc Willelmi comitis Sar' Willelmi comitis Warenn' Willelmi comitis Arundell' Alani de Galweya constabularii Scottie Warini filii Geroldi Huberti de Burgo senescalli Pictavie Petri filii Hereberti Hugonis de Nevill' Mathei filii Hereberti Thome Basset Alani Basset Philippi de Alben' Roberti de Roppel' Johannis Mariscalli Johannis filii Hugonis et aliorum fidelium nostrorum In primis concessisse Deo et hac presenti carta nostra confirmasse pro nobis et heredibus nostris in perpetuum quod Anglicana ecclesia libera sit et habeat iura sua integra et libertates suas illesas et ita volumus observari quod apparet ex eo quod libertatem electionum que maxima et magis necessaria reputatur ecclesie Anglicane mera et spontanea voluntate ante discordiam inter nos et barones nostros motam concessimus et carta nostra confirmavimus et eam optinuimus a domino papa Innocentio tercio confirmari quam et nos observabimus et ab heredibus nostris in perpetuum bona fide volumus observari Concessimus etiam omnibus liberis hominibus regni nostri pro nobis et heredibus nostris in perpetuum omnes libertates subscriptas habendas et tenendas eis et heredibus suis de nobis et

In 1832, when the Law Library was established as a separate department of the Library of Congress, its collections included just over two thousand volumes, 639 of which had been part of Thomas Jefferson's library. The photograph above shows the space occupied by the Law Library when it was located in the Capitol. Now in the Madison Building, the Law Library holds over two million items, from the mundane to the magnificent—including the Magna Carta, at left, printed in gold letters with watercolor initials in London in 1816.

through copyright deposit—maps, music, and graphic arts. Spofford's successors as Librarian of Congress hired subject specialists to develop these and other collections and persuaded Congress to begin appropriating substantial funds for the purchase of research materials for all collections. Today, copyright is still one of the Library's major acquisitions sources, but between the years 1865 and 1897, it played a crucial role in the development of the Library of Congress into a national institution.

The copyright law of 1870 had another major effect: it forced the construction of a building for the Library. Spofford foresaw this result almost immediately. In his 1871 annual report he suggested that a separate building might be needed because of the increased receipts resulting from the new copyright law. The next year he presented a plan for such a building, initiating an endeavor that soon dominated his librarianship. In the twenty-five year struggle to make the building a reality, Spofford enlisted the support of many powerful public figures: congressmen, cultural leaders, journalists, and even presidents. The speeches and statements he elicited usually endorsed not only a separate building, but also the concept of the Library of Congress as a national library.

Spofford's most dependable supporters were two senators, both personal friends and frequent users of his Library: Justin S. Morrill of Vermont and Daniel W. Voorhees of Indiana. In March 1879, Morrill delivered a major speech in which he strongly endorsed a separate Library building and Spofford's national library concept:

We must either reduce the Library to the stinted and specific wants of Congress alone, or permit it to advance to national importance, and give it room equal to the culture, wants, and resources of a great people. The higher education of our common country demands that this institution shall not be crippled for lack of room.[5]

Senator Voorhees, chairman of the Joint Committee on the Library, was more passionate. In a May 1880 speech, he expressed his very Jeffersonian belief in the essential moral value of books and intellectual activity:

Let us therefore give this great national library our love and our care. Nothing can surpass it in importance. Knowledge is power, the power to maintain free government and preserve constitutional liberty. Without it the world grows dark and the human race takes up its backward race to the regions of barbarism. I cannot believe that the plain and imperative duty of Congress on the subject of its Library will be longer neglected.[6]

Such eloquence, plus behind-the-scenes efforts by Morrill, Voorhees, and Spofford, finally resulted in 1886 in authorization for a structure directly across the east plaza from the Capitol. After further delays, construction be-

A wonderful collaboration among architects, craftsmen, artists, and workmen, the first Library of Congress building was authorized in 1886 and completed in 1897. Among the important steps in its construction was the placing of the keystone in the southwest clerestory arch, memorialized here in a photograph from the Prints and Photographs Division.

gan in earnest in 1889 and the new building, opened to the public in 1897, was immediately hailed as a national monument. Now called the Thomas Jefferson Building, this imposing structure in the style of the Italian Renaissance, with its grand Main Reading Room at the center and exuberant interior decoration throughout, is an incomparable symbol of the universality of knowledge.

To Spofford also goes primary credit for beginning the Library's tradition of broad public service. In 1865 he extended the hours of service, so that the Library was open every weekday all year. In 1869 he began advocating evening hours, but this innovation was not approved by Congress until 1898. Finally, in 1870 Spofford reinstated the earlier policy of lending books directly to the public if an appropriate sum was left on deposit, a procedure that remained in effect until 1894, when preparations were started for the move into the new Library building.

In 1896, just before the actual move, the Joint Library Committee held hearings about "the condition" of the Library and its possible reorganization. The hearings provided an occasion for a detailed examination of the Library's history and present functions and for a review of what new functions the Library might perform once it occupied the spacious new building. The American Library Association sent six witnesses, including future Librarian of Congress Herbert Putnam from the Boston Public Library and Melvil Dewey

The Library's Fine Prints Collection spans four centuries and includes the work of artists from many countries. Housed in the Prints and Photographs Division, the collection is among the world's largest, containing some 100,000 images including woodcuts, engravings, etchings, lithographs, silkscreens, and other graphic media. Battle of the Fish, *the hand-colored woodcut reproduced above, is by German master Max Ernst (1891–1976). An earlier German master,* Hieronymous Hopfer *(floruit 1520–1535) created the etching of a peasant couple dancing, at right, after an engraving by Albrecht Dürer.*

Among the approximately eight hundred tons of books, pamphlets, maps, manuscripts, prints, pieces of music, and other materials moved into the first Library of Congress building in 1897 were these copyright deposits, photographed as they were waiting to be sorted, counted, and classified.

from the New York State Library. Members of Congress listened with great interest to the testimony of Putnam and Dewey, who argued that the national services of the Library should be greatly expanded. Dewey felt that the Library of Congress now had the opportunity to act as a true national library, which he defined as "a center to which the libraries of the whole country can turn for inspiration, guidance, and practical help, which can be rendered so economically and efficiently in no other possible way."[7]

Testimony at the 1896 hearings greatly influenced the reorganization of the Library, which was incorporated into the Legislative Appropriations Act approved February 19, 1897, and became effective on July 1, 1897. In accordance with the recommendations of Spofford, Putnam, Dewey, and the other officials who testified, all phases of the Library's activities were expanded. The size of the staff was increased from 42 to 108, and new administrative units were established for the reading room, the art gallery (graphic arts), maps and charts, and the cataloging, copyright, manuscripts, music, and periodicals departments. During his thirty-two years in office, and with the consent of the Joint Library Committee, Librarian Spofford had assumed full responsibility for directing the Library's affairs. This authority formally passed to the office of Librarian of Congress in the 1897 reorganization, for the Librarian explicitly was assigned sole responsibility for making the "rules and regulations for the government" of the Library, including the selection of its staff. The same reorganization act stipulated that the president's appointment of a Librarian of Congress thereafter was to be approved by the Senate.

Pres. William McKinley appointed a new Librarian of Congress to supervise the move from the Capitol and implement the new reorganization. He was John Russell Young, who held office briefly, from July 1, 1897, until his death in January 1899. A journalist and former diplomat, Young was a skilled administrator who worked hard to strengthen both the comprehensiveness of the collections and the scope of the services provided to Congress. He honored Jefferson's influence on the Library, bringing Jefferson's books into a special room and commissioning a report on the Jefferson library that was published in the Library's 1898 annual report.

Young used his diplomatic ties and experience to enlarge the Library's collections. In February 1898, for example, he sent a letter to U.S. diplomatic and consular representatives throughout the world, asking them to send "to the national library" newspapers, journals, pamphlets, manuscripts, broadsides, "documents illustrative of the history of those various nationalities now coming to our shores to blend into our national life," and other categories of research materials, broadly summarized as "whatever, in a word, would add to the sum of human knowledge." By the end of 1898, books and other materials had been received from eleven legations and seven consulates.

Young skillfully guided the administrative reorganization. He made many important professional appointments, including Thorvald Solberg, the first register of copyrights, and catalogers J. C. M. Hanson and Charles Martel, who began reclassifying the collections after nearly a century of reliance on the classification scheme Thomas Jefferson provided to the Library along with his books. While himself a political appointee, Young was nonpartisan in his appointments and successfully distanced the Library of Congress from the world of partisan politics.

Young also inaugurated what today is one of the Library's best known national activities, library service for the blind and physically handicapped. In November of 1897 the Library began a program of daily readings for the blind in a special "pavilion for the blind" complete with its own library. In 1913 Congress directed the American Printing House for the Blind to begin depositing embossed books in the Library, and in 1931 a separate appropriation was authorized for providing "books for the use of adult blind residents of the United States."

Herbert Putnam, Young's successor, was appointed by President McKinley in the spring of 1899 and served as Librarian of Congress for forty years, until the autumn of 1939. Asked to characterize the Library as he neared the end of his long career, Putnam penned the phrase "Universal in Scope: National in Service." This view marked his entire tenure, for if Spofford was the principal collection-builder, Putnam was the Librarian who did the most to extend the Library's use to the American people. He created a systematic program of widespread public use that exists to this day, opening up the collections to scholars, the public, and to other libraries. The first experienced librarian to serve as Librarian of Congress, Putnam established a working partnership between the Library of Congress and the American library movement. Rather than serving merely as a great national accumulation of books, a national library should, he felt, actively serve other libraries.

In the quarter century before Putnam took office, a new structure of scientific and scholarly activity had evolved rapidly in the United States. Professional schools and new universities offering graduate work were established; numerous professional associations and societies came into existence; and the federal government became an active supporter of education, research, and scientific activity. By 1900, the age of the great library had arrived in America; its characteristics included huge bookstacks, scientific cataloging and classification, and full-time professional staffs.

By the end of 1901 the Library of Congress, the first American library to reach one million volumes, had started organizing its enormous collections of recorded knowledge for public service and become the leader among American libraries.

Putnam's actions in 1901 were imaginative and decisive and were approved by both the Joint Library Committee and the professional library community. In that year, for example, the first volume of a completely new classification scheme, based on the Library's own collections, was published; access to the Library was extended to "scientific investigators and duly qualified individuals" throughout the United States; an interlibrary loan service was inaugurated; and the sale and distribution of Library of Congress printed catalog cards began.

The interlibrary loan system established by Putnam in 1901 was a radical step, for it signaled the institution's transition from a national storehouse of books to a national laboratory or workshop for promoting the use of its collections. When asked to defend his position of sending books outside the Library, the Librarian explained that the risk was worth it because "a book used, is after all, fulfilling a higher mission than a book which is merely being preserved for possible future use."[8]

Librarian Putnam's extension of the Library's classification and cataloging schemes to the rest of the nation helped "democratize" knowledge, nationally and internationally, for it established bibliographic standards and encouraged cooperative endeavors among librarians and scholars. This sharing of the Library's "bibliographic apparatus" helped shape and systematize intellectual activity in America and propelled the Library of Congress into a position of leadership among the world's research institutions.[9]

The development of the Library's collections into a nationally useful resource took many forms. To aid historical research, Putnam felt that the national library "should be able to offer original sources" about the national life.[10] In 1903, he persuaded his friend and supporter, Pres. Theodore Roo-

"Father of the Constitution" James Madison took these notes July 14, 1787, as the Constitutional Convention debated the provisions of the document which has proven a sturdy foundation for the government of the United States for over two hundred years. Part of the James Madison Papers in the Manuscript Division, the notes attest to Madison's profound intellectual contributions to the new country.

Monday May 28. —

From Mass^{ts} Nat: Gorham & Caleb Strong took their seats. From Connecticut Oliver Elsworth

From Delaware Gunning Bedford. From Maryland James McHenry. From Penn^a B. Franklin George

Mr Wythe from the Committee for preparing rules made report which employed the deliberations of this

day:

Mr King objected to one of the rules in the Report authorizing any member to call for

the yeas & nays and have them entered on the minutes. He urged that it was unnecessary

as the acts of the Convention were not to bind the Constituents, & exhibit this evidence of the

votes; and improper as changes of opinion would be frequent in the course of the business

would

& fill the minutes with contradictions.

Col. seconded the objection; adding that such a record of the opinions of members

would be obstacle to a change of them on conviction; and in case of its being hereafter promul-

ged would furnish a handle to the adversaries of the Result of the Meeting

The proposed rule was rejected nem. contrad. vote. The standing rules agreed to

were as follow [See the Journal] & copy here the printed rules

The Rule restraining members from communicating the proceedings of the Con-

vention &c. was agreed to nem. con. for reasons similar to those abovementioned.

[illegible] the Rules being dispensed to, the rest [illegible]

[illegible] follow [illegible] Note B

A letter from sundry persons of the State of Rho. Island addressed

to the Honorable The Chairman of the General Convention was presented to the

chair by Mr Govr Morris, and being read was ordered to lie on the

table for further consideration. [For the letter see Note C in the appendix]

Mr Butler moved that the House provide agst interruption of

business by absence of members, and against licentious publications of their

which

proceedings — to was added by — Mr Spaight a motion to provide that

on the one hand the House might not be precluded by a vote upon any

question, from revising the subject matter of it, when they see cause, nor, on

the other hand, be led too hastily to rescind a decision, which was the result

of mature discussion. Whereupon it was ordered that these questions be refer-

red to the consideration of the Committee appointed to draw up the Standing rules

and that the Committee make report thereon. adj^d till tom^w at 10. O'clock

sevelt, to issue an executive order that transferred the papers of many of the nation's founding fathers, including George Washington, Thomas Jefferson, and James Madison, from the State Department archives to the Library's Manuscript Division. In 1904, the Library began publishing important historical texts from its collections, such as the *Journals of the Continental Congress*. Putnam felt the publication of such manuscripts was "not perhaps so much a service from us as a library as a duty from us as the custodians of original sources for American history."

As American influence and interests began to expand in the twentieth century, Putnam looked abroad to build the Library's collections, boldly applying Jefferson's dictum that no subject was beyond the possible concern of Congress or the American people. The Librarian was especially farsighted in acquiring research materials about other countries and cultures. In 1904 he purchased a four thousand volume library of Indica, explaining in the Library's annual report that he "could not ignore the opportunity to acquire a unique collection which scholarship thought worthy of prolonged, scientific, and enthusiastic research, even though the immediate use of such a collection may prove meager." In 1906 he acquired the famous eighty thousand volume private library of Russian literature owned by G. V. Yudin of Siberia, even sending a staff member to Russia to supervise the packing and shipping of the books. The Schatz collection of early opera librettos was purchased from a German collector in 1908. Large and important collections of Hebraica and Chinese and Japanese books also were acquired.

In one notable instance, Congress took the initiative in building the Library's collections. In December 1929, ignoring the stock market crash two months earlier, Congressman Ross Collins of Mississippi proposed the purchase for $1.5 million of the three thousand volume collection of early books assembled by collector Otto F. Vollbehr, which included one of three perfect existing vellum copies of the Gutenberg Bible. Congressman Albert Johnson of Washington, in the debate in the House of Representatives, maintained that "even if times are hard," Congress should purchase the collection because "it is all for the United States of America which is going to live we hope for thousands of years." Putnam, testifying before the Senate Library Committee, added his endorsement to the enthusiasm expressed by the House of Representatives. He reminded the committee that in 1815, the government paid Thomas Jefferson nearly $24,000 for his library, and "in proportion to the resources of the country that sum was not much short of the million and a half" asked for the Vollbehr collection. Moreover, "what was true of that purchase is certainly true of the one before you. It would form 'a most admirable substratum for a (greater) national library.'" The purchase was approved in 1930 and Putnam went to Europe to bring the Gutenberg Bible to American shores.[11]

In the early 1930s, 2,600 volumes from the book collections of the Romanov family were purchased by the Library. The Russian Imperial Collection includes biographies, works of literature, and military, social, and administrative histories, held chiefly in the Rare Book and Special Collections Division. The Law Library, however, received copies of military and civil law books, some of which are pictured at left. The ornate pink volume probably belonged to Catherine the Great.

The Library's foremost function, support for the legislature, was strengthened in 1914 when the Legislative Reference Service was established as a separate administrative unit. Its creation was a natural development in the progressive era, when many people in business and public life advocated the "scientific" (and Jeffersonian) use of information to solve problems. Specialized library units for legislative research were established in several states, notably Wisconsin, during the early 1900s. By the second decade of the century, the legislative reference movement reached the national legislature. In his 1913 testimony before the Senate, Putnam explained the function of the proposed legislative reference bureau within the Library:

What we do not do, and what a legislative reference division in the Library would do, is to select out of this great collection—now 2,000,000 books and pamphlets—the material that may bear upon one or another of the topics under consideration by Congress or that are likely to be under consideration, or that come up under particular discussions.[12]

In other words, the Library would begin providing the Congress a *research* service. In 1915 the Librarian reported that the new legislative service was anticipating questions from Congress on: "the conservation bills, so-called," the merchant marine, the government of the Philippines, immigration, convict-made goods, railroad securities, federal aid in roadmaking, publicity in campaign contributions, and a national budget system.[13]

While enhancing established functions Putnam also moved the Library in new directions. A major avenue for the Librarian's innovations was the Library of Congress Trust Fund Board Act of 1925, which enabled the institution to accept gifts and bequests from private citizens. This legislation created a new cultural role for the Library.

A proposal from a private citizen, Elizabeth Sprague Coolidge, led directly to the creation of the Trust Fund Board. She offered an endowment to the Library for promoting the appreciation and understanding of music. She also offered to pay for a concert hall within the Library's building, to support the commissioning of new works of music, and to provide the chief of the Music Division with a generous honorarium. Prominent individuals such as James B. Wilbur, Archer Huntington, John D. Rockefeller, Gertrude Clarke Whittall, and many others soon joined Mrs. Coolidge as Library of Congress benefactors. In particular, Gertrude Clarke Whittall's donation of five Stradivari instruments and the funding for concerts at which they could be played helped establish the Library as a patron of the arts. (Her gift also was a particularly appropriate one for the Library, as Thomas Jefferson's legacy includes an informed appreciation for the fine arts, and he himself played the violin and the cello.) This new private funding through the Trust Fund also allowed the Library to establish chairs and consultantships for scholars and

One of three perfect vellum copies of the Gutenberg Bible, shown in detail at right, came to the Library of Congress in 1930, after Congress approved acquisition of the Vollbehr collection of incunabula (items printed between 1450 and 1500). Among the Library's greatest treasures, the Bible represents one of the world's most astonishing technological inventions— the technique of printing by individual, movable pieces of type.

qua cum plerasq̃ uellis
undere esse descripsos me
rito estimar apud he
breos ligaric et in psalmis
uel opusculis salomonis.

N Sed qꝥ in demosthene et tullio solet he
ri ut in psola scribant et in comata sco
tas prosa et non uersibus cõscripserit.
nos quoqꝫ utilitati legentiu prouidentes.
interptationem nouam nouo scribendi
genere distinximus. At primu in uos disceru
la scienduꝫ qꝥ in sermone nobilis et urbane se
sit quippe ut uir nobilis quiꝗqua in eloquio
pganus: nec habes quicqua. Unde accidit.
rusticanis animaꝫ. Denuo etiaꝫ
ut pre terreis flore suonie. Denuo etiaꝫ prophetia
no non potuerit cõseruare. Jtaꝗ uni
dicendꝰ sit ꝗ euangelista. mysteria ad loqui
futuro uatemari. Unde conicio nolui sir hi
siꝗpte septuaginta interptes ꝓ
ne sacerdum canibꝪ: et margaritas legeris
ne terrear: que cu hanc editione absconditra.
sie ab illis animaduerteret pot
sier ignoro quaꝫ labore sir prophe
tras intelligere: nec facile quempiam
posse iudicare de interptatione: uin
intellegeret ante que legerit. flos qꝫ pa
ne moestos plurimoꝫ: qui siimilar
re inuidia qꝥ cõsequi non ualet a litauis
nut. Seires rego et prudes i flaua
in manu: et nichilominus precor: ut quo
sie lectoribꝪ precor: ut quo
post septuaginta tralatore
lymachu et theodotione cõpar
nu uoleine sic. et collatione
magis se collatione

The genius of John Philip Sousa, America's beloved March King, is celebrated in this collection of items from the Music Division. Displayed at left are a photo of the sixty-piece Sousa Band during the 1920 season tour, the 1901 piano version of The Invincible Eagle *march, and a souvenir program from the 1926 band tour. The piccolo, from the Dayton C. Miller Flute Collection, was made circa 1897 for Frank Wadsworth, a flutist in the Sousa Band. And the French cornet from the R. E. Sheldon Wind Instrument Collection is typical of those used in Sousa's band at the turn of the century.*

a consultantship for poetry, which has evolved today into the Poet Laureate Consultant in Poetry.

Putnam was careful in defining the use of the support the Library received through the Trust Fund. Private funds were to serve a limited role, to "do for American scholarship and cultivation what is not likely to be done by other agencies" and most definitely supplement, not replace, the annual government appropriation.[14] His vision for the Library's cultural and educational role and how it could be developed and funded established a precedent for the valuable private sector support that the Library of Congress receives today.

The Library's symbolic role as a cradle of Jeffersonian democracy was enhanced by Putnam in 1921 when, at his behest, the nation's two most precious documents, the Declaration of Independence and the Constitution, were transferred to the Library from the State Department. In 1924 the documents went on permanent public display in a specially designed "Shrine" in the Library's Great Hall. Pres. Calvin Coolidge and many other dignitaries took part in the ceremony, but there were no speeches, only the singing of two stanzas of "America." The Library transferred both documents to the National Archives in 1952, but still holds, as one of its greatest treasures, Jefferson's handwritten draft of the Declaration of Independence. And the spirit behind that great document pervades the Library. In his book *The Epic of America*, published in 1931, historian James Truslow Adams paid tribute to the Library of Congress "as a symbol of what democracy can accomplish on its own behalf . . . founded and built by the people, it is for the people."[15]

The expansion of the Library's collections and services during Putnam's forty years as Librarian naturally required additional space. Additional bookstacks within the Jefferson Building were built in 1910 and 1927. In 1907, Putnam had assured Congress that when the shelving space in the Jefferson Building was gone, "storage shelving may be extended into plain, simple, inexpensive but appropriate buildings in the neighborhood." Legislation to acquire land for a new structure was approved in 1928, and the Annex Building (today the Adams Building) was authorized in 1930. Construction was delayed during the Depression years, but the classically simple and rectangular structure was completed in 1938 and opened to the public in 1939.

The Library of Congress as a democratic institution and repository of American cultural traditions was a concept that captured the imagination of Putnam's successor, writer and poet Archibald MacLeish. Appointed by Pres. Franklin Roosevelt in 1939, MacLeish served as Librarian of Congress until the end of 1944, when he became assistant secretary of state. An advocate of U.S. involvement in World War II, MacLeish used the office of Librarian of Congress to speak out on behalf of democracy. He urged librarians to "become active and not passive agents of the democratic process," and criticized his fellow intellectuals for their failure to defend American culture against the threat of totalitarianism. He became the most visible Librarian of Congress in the history of the office.

Thomas Jefferson's concept of liberty and self-government inspired Librarian MacLeish who, in 1941, dedicated the South Reading Room in the Adams Building to the Library's principal founder. At MacLeish's request, artist Ezra Winter decorated the Jefferson Reading Room with four murals that drew their theme from quotations from Jefferson on the subjects of freedom, labor, the "living generation," education, and democratic government. MacLeish established a "democracy alcove" in the Main Reading Room, where readers could find "the classic texts of the American tradition," including the Declaration of Independence, the Constitution, the Federalist Papers, and other writings of American statesmen.

In 1943, the Library commemorated the bicentennial of Jefferson's birth. In opening the Library's exhibit, MacLeish called Jefferson's definition of liberty the "greatest and the most moving, as it is the most articulate." An annotated catalog of the books in Jefferson's personal library by bibliographer E. Millicent Sowerby was undertaken (it was published in five volumes, 1952–59), and the Library started microfilming its collection of Jefferson papers in the same year.

Thanks to MacLeish's personal interest and contacts, during his librarianship the Library of Congress established new and enduring relationships with American writers and scholars. Other highlights of the fruitful MacLeish years included the development of Library-wide objectives; an administrative reorganization so thorough that it lasted for more than three decades; the creation of a rotating consultantship in poetry; and fellowship programs for young scholars. The Librarian articulated Jefferson's rationale as it applied to foreign materials, asserting, in his "Canons of Selection" in his 1940 annual report, that the Library should acquire the "written records of those societies and peoples whose experience is of most immediate concern to the people of the United States." Indeed, World War II's most important effect on the Library was to stimulate further development of its collections about other nations.

Librarian MacLeish resigned in 1944 and, in 1945, Pres. Harry Truman named assistant librarian Luther H. Evans, a political scientist, as Librarian. Evans served until 1953. To justify his ambitious proposals in fiscal year 1947 to expand the Library's collections and services, Evans emphasized Jefferson's "doctrine of completeness and inclusiveness." The challenges of the postwar years meant, to Evans, that "no spot on the earth's surface is any longer alien to the interest of the American people." He felt that the major lesson of World War II was that "however large our collections may now be, they are pitifully and tragically small in comparison with the demands of the nation." He described the need for larger collections of research materials about foreign

In September 1944, Librarian of Congress Archibald MacLeish, center, joined Reference Department director David C. Mearns and Verner W. Clapp, director of the Acquisitions Department in examining Thomas Jefferson's rough draft of the Declaration of Independence. The Declaration and other muniments had just been returned to the Library from safekeeping at Fort Knox.

countries in practical, patriotic terms, noting that in the years leading up to the war "the want of early issues of the *Voelkische Beobachter* prevented the first auguries of Naziism," while during the war, weather data on the Himalayas from the Library's collections helped the Air Force.[16]

The acquisitions, cataloging, and bibliographic services of the Library grew during the Evans years, but not as rapidly as the Librarian would have liked. He believed that the Library of Congress should actively serve all libraries, but an economy-minded postwar Congress balked at his expansionist plans. Evans's leadership and energy helped compensate for the lack of large budget increases, however. Cooperative projects in acquiring and cataloging materials were undertaken regionally and nationally. His strong personal interest in issues such as copyright and intellectual freedom strengthened the Library's involvement in each of these areas.

A new Library of Congress commitment to international library and cultural cooperation was one of Evans's major contributions.[17] The Library of Congress Mission in Europe, organized by Evans and director of acquisitions Verner W. Clapp in 1945, acquired European publications for the Library and for other American libraries. The Library soon initiated automatic book purchase agreements with foreign dealers around the world and greatly expanded its agreements for the international exchange of official publications. It organized a reference library in San Francisco in 1945 to assist the participants in the meeting that established the United Nations. In 1947, a Library of Congress Mission to Japan provided advice for the establishment of the National Diet Library. Evans also believed strongly in cultural reparation: that original source materials belonged in the country of their creation. As Librarian of Congress, he initiated the return of several important manuscripts from the Library to the countries of their origin.

Evans's successor as Librarian of Congress was L. Quincy Mumford, who was director of the Cleveland Public Library in 1954 when he was nominated by Pres. Dwight D. Eisenhower. Mumford, who in 1957 initiated the planning that led to the construction of the Madison Building, guided the Library through its most intensive period of national and international expansion. In the 1960s the Library of Congress benefited from increased federal funding for education, libraries, and research. Most dramatic was the growth of the foreign acquisitions program, an expansion based on Evans's achievements a decade earlier. In 1958 the Library was authorized by Congress to acquire books by using U.S.-owned foreign currency under the terms of the Agricultural Trade Development and Assistance Act of 1954 (Public Law 480). The first appropriation for this purpose was made in 1961, enabling the Library to establish acquisitions centers in New Delhi and Cairo to purchase publications and distribute them to research libraries throughout the United States. This, however, was only the first step.

In 1965, Pres. Lyndon B. Johnson approved a Higher Education Act which, through Title IIC, had great significance for the Library of Congress and for academic and research libraries throughout the nation. The new law authorized the Office of Education to transfer funds to the Library of Congress for the ambitious purposes of acquiring, insofar as possible, all current library materials of value to scholarship published throughout the world, and providing cataloging information for these materials promptly after they had been received. This law came closer than any other legislation to making Jefferson's concept of comprehensiveness part of the Library's official mandate. The new effort was christened the National Program for Acquisitions and Cataloging (NPAC). The first NPAC office was opened in London in 1966. In the past decade the Library's overseas operations have been consolidated. Today, the Library has six overseas offices and cooperative acquisitions arrangements with booksellers and libraries around the world.

Shared acquisitions and cataloging made international bibliographic standards imperative. The crucial development took place at the Library of Congress in the mid-1960s: the creation of the Library of Congress MARC (Machine Readable Cataloging) format for communicating bibliographic data in machine-readable form. This new capability for converting, maintaining, and distributing bibliographic information soon became the standard format for sharing data about books and other research materials. The possibility of worldwide application was immediately recognized, and the MARC format structure became an official national standard in 1971 and an international standard in 1973.

The preservation and conservation of library collections has become an important concern of research libraries in the past few decades. In 1967, the Library of Congress inaugurated a pilot project to study techniques for the preservation of deteriorating or "brittle" books—volumes disintegrating because they were printed on acidic paper. Today, the Library's Preservation Office administers this nation's largest library research and conservation effort.

The Mumford administration, a period of rapid growth, was also the last time there was serious public debate about the dual legislative and national roles of the Library of Congress. The Library of Congress has played a leadership role in the American library community since 1901; however, its *first* responsibility, as part of the legislative branch of the American government, always has been to support the reference and research needs of the American national legislature. In spite of the impressive list of "national library functions" it performs, the Library of Congress is not the official National Library of the United States or even necessarily the center of American library and information activities.

In 1962, at the request of Sen. Claiborne Pell of the Joint Library Committee, Douglas Bryant, associate director of the Harvard University Library prepared a memorandum on "what the Library of Congress does and ought to do for the Government and the Nation generally." Bryant urged further expansion of the Library's national activities and services, proposals endorsed by many professional librarians, and suggested several organizational changes. Mumford replied to the Bryant memorandum in his 1962 annual report, strongly defending the Library's position in the legislative branch and stating his opposition to the suggestion in the report that the Library's name might be altered to reflect its national role: "The Library of Congress is a venerable institution, with a proud history, and to change its name would do unspeakable violence to tradition."

The debate continued in the professional library community. However, the fiscal retrenchments of the 1970s and a reemphasis of the Library's legislative services under the provisions of the Legislative Reorganization Act of 1970 rendered any increased national library aspirations impractical. The new law changed the name of the Legislative Reference Service to the Congressional Research Service and expanded its functions, placing increased emphasis on policy research and analysis and on direct services to both individual members of Congress and congressional committees.

Librarian Mumford retired in 1974. In 1975, Pres. Gerald R. Ford nominated historian Daniel J. Boorstin, who had been director of the Smithsonian Institution's National Museum of History and Technology (now American History), to be the twelfth Librarian of Congress. Boorstin was confirmed by the Senate and took the oath of office on November 12, 1975, in a ceremony in the Library's Great Hall.

Boorstin immediately faced two major challenges: the need to review the Library's organization and functions and, pending the forthcoming expansion into the James Madison Memorial Building, the lack of space for both collections and staff. In 1976, he created a Task Force on Goals, Organization, and Planning, a staff group which conducted, with help from outside advisers, a one-year review of the Library and its role. Many of the task force's recommendations were incorporated into a subsequent reorganization.[18] The move into the Madison Building, which began in 1980 and was completed in 1982, relieved administrative as well as physical pressures, and enabled Librarian Boorstin to focus on what he deemed most important: the strengthening of the Library's ties to Congress, and the development of new relationships between the Library and scholars, authors, publishers, cultural leaders, and the business community.

The Library of Congress grew steadily during Boorstin's administration, with its annual appropriation increasing from $116 million in 1975 to more than $250 million in 1987, even though the Gramm-Rudman-Hollings budget restrictions slowed growth severely in 1985 and 1986. Like MacLeish, Boorstin relied heavily on his professional staff in technical areas such as cataloging, automation, and library preservation. But he took a keen personal interest in collection development; in copyright; in book and reading promotion; in the symbolic role of the Library of Congress in American life; and in the Library as "the world's greatest Multi-Media Encyclopedia." Boorstin's style and accomplishments increased the visibility of the Library to the point where in January 1987 a *New York Times* reporter, discussing Boorstin's decision to retire as Librarian, called the post of Librarian of Congress "perhaps the leading intellectual public position in the nation."

Boorstin's successor, historian James H. Billington, was nominated by Pres. Ronald Reagan and took the oath of office as the thirteenth Librarian of Congress on September 14, 1987. Billington immediately took personal charge of the Library, instituting his own one-year review through a Management and Planning (MAP) Committee, a process that included regional forums in nine cities. The result was a major administrative reorganization based on goals identified through the MAP study.[19] Convinced that the Library of Congress needed to share its resources throughout the nation more widely, he instituted several projects to test new technologies that might extend direct access by libraries and schools to the Library's collections and data bases. The experimental American Memory project, for example, provides electronic copies of selected collections of American history and culture to schools and libraries. A two-year pilot project providing on-line access to the Library to the fifty state library agencies began in 1991.

Envisioning a new educational role for the Library, Billington began strengthening the Library's cultural programming and established its first Education Office. Recognition of the crucial importance of private funds in building and sustaining national outreach projects led to the creation of a Development Office in 1988. The establishment in 1990 of the James Madison Council, a private-sector support body consisting mostly of business executives and entrepreneurs, brought new support. In fiscal 1991, Billington obtained a 12 percent budget increase for the Library to help make its collections more accessible. New initiatives also provided Library of Congress guidance to parliamentary libraries in the newly emerging democracies of Eastern Europe.

In his budget presentation to Congress for fiscal year 1993, Billington emphasized how the Library of Congress is "becoming an even more important catalyst for the educational, competitive, and creative needs of our nation." The complexities of today's information age, particularly when compared to the relatively simple demands faced by the Library in Thomas Jefferson's time, were most apparent in the Librarian's discussion of new electronic technology. Yet the new technology, "properly organized and supported" will, according to Billington, be applied to a Jeffersonian purpose, enabling the Library to "increase the knowledge available to Americans in their local communities—in schools, colleges, libraries, and private sector research enterprises." Thus, "even those Americans far from great universities and the most affluent schools and libraries can still have access to the best of the nation's heritage and the latest in up-to-date information."[20]

In his Sixth Annual Message as president, Thomas Jefferson proposed the creation of a national university, because "a public institution alone can supply those sciences which, though rarely called for, are yet necessary to complete the circle, all the parts of which contribute to the improvement of the country."[21] Billington's efforts to exploit new electronic technologies and educational partnerships, governmental and private, present the intriguing possibility of the Library of Congress, nearly two centuries after Jefferson's proposal, becoming the core of a new "Electronic National University."

Librarian Billington's determination to extend the reach and influence of the Library of Congress is very much in the ambitious tradition of his predecessors. Alone among the world's great libraries, the Library of Congress still attempts to be a universal library, collecting printed materials in almost all languages and nonprint materials in almost all media. As it approaches its bicentennial in the year 2000, it still is guided by Thomas Jefferson's beliefs that democracy depends on knowledge and that all topics are important to the library of the American national legislature—and therefore to the American people.

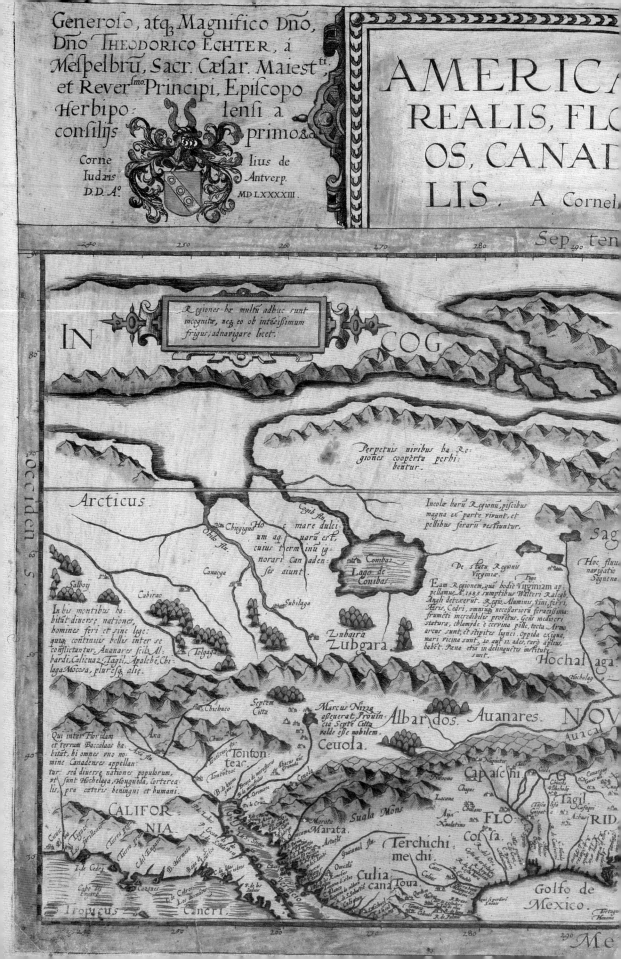

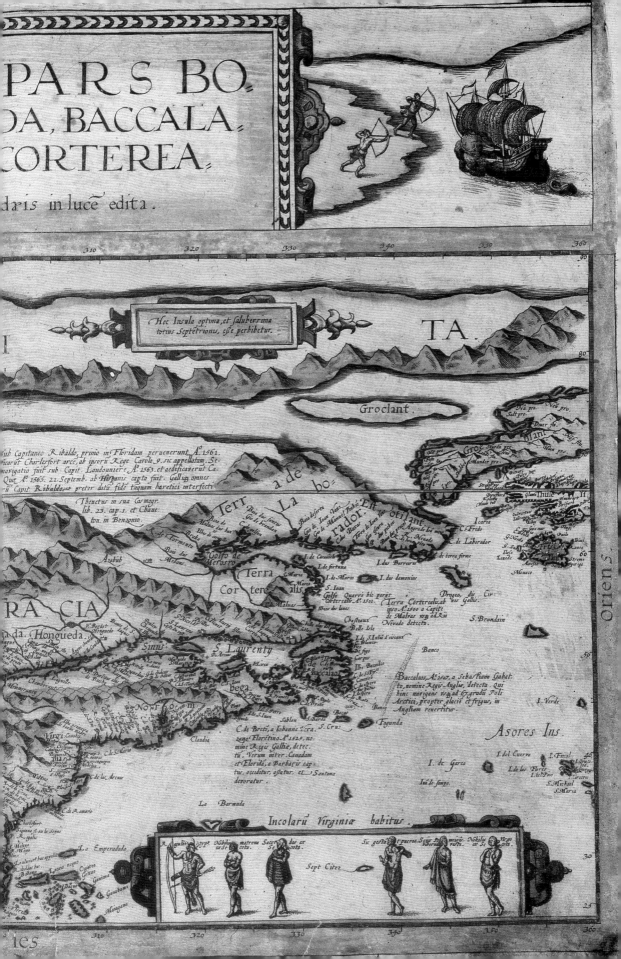

PARS BOREA, BACCALAORTEREA,

Incolarū Virginiæ habitus.

Cattleya labiata.

The Collections

Depictions of the world and its wonders: The rendering of Cattleya Labiata, *at left, is from Conrad Loddiges & Sons'* The Botanical Cabinet, *published in London between 1817 and 1833, and located in the Rare Book and Special Collections Division. The Geography and Map Division holds the map of North America, pages 42–43. Engraved by Dutch map publisher Cornelis de Jode in 1578, it is one of the earliest maps reflecting expedition-ers' reports.*

The enormous size and variety of its collections make the Library of Congress the largest library in the world. True to the Jeffersonian ideal, the collections are comprehensive in scope, including research materials in more than 450 languages and in many media.

The growth of the collections is relentless. Materials come to the Library through an acquisitions program that extends throughout the world and includes over fifteen thousand agreements with foreign governments and research institutions for the exchange of research materials; gifts; purchases; transfers from other U.S. government agencies; and copyright deposits. Each day about thirty-one thousand items arrive at the Library; approximately seven thousand of these items will become part of the permanent collections. The Library, however, defers to the National Library of Medicine and the National Agricultural Library for intensive collecting in the fields of clinical medicine and technical agriculture, respectively.

In 1992, the Library acquired its 100 millionth item. The collections now include approximately fifteen million books, thirty-nine million manuscripts, thirteen million photographs, four million maps, more than three and a half million pieces of music, and more than half a million motion pictures. The Library's collection of more than 5,600 incunabula (books printed before 1500) is the largest in the Western Hemisphere and its collections of maps, atlases, newspapers, music, motion pictures, photographs, and microforms are probably the largest in the world. In addition, the Library holds newspapers, prints, posters, drawings, talking books, technical reports, videotapes and disks, computer programs, and other audio, visual, and print materials.

The collections are especially strong in American history, politics, and literature; music; geography; law and particularly foreign law; economics; genealogy and U.S. local history; U.S. public documents; publications of learned societies from around the world; the history of science; libraries and librarianship; and bibliography in all subjects. In addition to the personal papers of American presidents from Washington through Coolidge, the Library's manuscript holdings include the papers of eminent figures, mostly American, in government, the arts, and the sciences.

One would expect the Library of Congress to be strong in Americana, but many of its foreign language collections also are exceptional. Foreign newspapers and gazettes are a special strength; for example, the Library acquires fourteen newspapers from Cuba, twenty from Romania, and eleven from Thailand. Moreover, approximately two-thirds of the books in its collections are in languages other than English. Its Chinese, Russian, Japanese, Korean, and Polish collections are the largest outside of those countries, and the Arabic collections are the largest outside of Egypt. Its collection of Luso-Hispanic materials is the largest in the world.

The resources of the Library of Congress, unique in scope and size, are organized into two major categories: the general or classified book and pamphlet collections, which are accessible through the Library's cataloging and retrieval system in the general reading rooms; and the special format, language, and subject collections, which are made available through a variety of cataloging and reference tools in specialized reading rooms, including a machine-readable collections reading room. Copyright deposits constitute the core of the general collections and many of the special collections, particularly the map, motion picture, music, photograph, and print collections.

The Library's role as a copyright depository has contributed to the popular belief that it contains one copy of every book published in the United States. It does not. Its collections are the most comprehensive in the country, but it is not a library of record in the legal sense; it is not required to retain all copyright deposits and, except for the period 1870–1909, it has never attempted to do so.

Historical highlights in the development of the Library's collections are presented below. The emphasis is on legislation, policies, and precedents that have shaped the growth of the collections and thus the services and activities of the entire Library. The acquisition of many of the Library's best-known collections also is noted.

1800

Pres. John Adams approves an act of Congress for the "accommodation of the Government of the United States" in the new capital city of Washington and the establishment of the Library of Congress.

1801

The first books, ordered from London, arrive and are stored in the Capitol. The collection consists of 740 volumes and three maps.

1802

The Library's first catalog is published. It lists the collection of 964 volumes according to their size and appends a list of nine maps and charts.

1806

Library Committee chairman Samuel Latham Mitchell, a senator from New York, urges the expansion of the Library: "Every week of the session causes additional regret that the volumes of literature and science within the reach of the national legislature are not more rich and ample."

1814

After capturing Washington, the British burn the U.S. Capitol, destroying the Library of Congress. Thomas Jefferson, in retirement at Monticello, offers to sell his personal library to the Library Committee of Congress in order to "recommence" the Congressional Library. He explains: "I do not know that it contains any branch of science which Congress would wish to exclude from their collection; there is, in fact, no subject to which a Member of Congress may not have occasion to refer."

1815

Pres. James Madison approves an act of Congress appropriating $23,950 for the acquisition of Jefferson's library of 6,487 volumes. The Library also adopts the classification scheme devised by Jefferson.

1824

The annual appropriation to the Library for the purchase of books is raised to $5,000.

1832

A separate "apartment" for the law collection is established, along with a separate appropriation for the purchase of law books.

"The Cathedral and the Leaning Tower of Pisa, Italy," above, is one of sixty hand-colored plates from Excursions Daguerriennes: Vues et Monuments les plus Remarquables du Globe, *1842, an extraordinary volume presenting early daguerreotype views from around the world, transferred onto copper plates and printed by letterpress. In the 1880s,* Photoglob of Zurich developed a prize-winning technique for adding color to black-and-white negatives and some of the results are shown at right. Both *Excursions* Daguerriennes *and the entire Photoglob output—some six thousand color photos of people and places around the world—are in the Prints and Photographs Division.*

1836

Addressing the American Historical Society, Secretary of War Lewis Cass advocates the expansion of the Library of Congress "in *all* the departments of human learning, as it will render it worthy of the age and country and elevate it to an equality with those great repositories of knowledge which are among the proudest ornaments of modern Europe."

1836

By a vote of seventeen to sixteen, the U.S. Senate rejects the purchase of the 25,000-volume Bourtoulin library, a rich collection of early Italian, Greek, and Latin works. The purchase was strongly recommended by Library Committee Chairman William Preston, senator from South Carolina, who cited Jefferson's "very wise and pointed statement that there is no subject to which a Member of Congress may not have occasion to refer."

Some of the most glorious treasures of the Library of Congress are in the custody of the Asian Division. Among them are early block-printed books, a scroll sutra from 975, pictographic manuscripts from southwestern China, and an example of Japanese printing dating from 770. The Mongolian Buddhist Sutra at left—an exquisite creation in pen, ink, gouache, and brocaded silk on paper—dates from the eighteenth century.

1837

The Library Committee authorizes the first exchange of official publications with foreign nations.

1846

The law establishing the Smithsonian Institution gives the Library of Congress, along with the Smithsonian, one copy of each copyrighted "book, map, chart, musical composition, print, cut, or engraving."

1851

A fire in the Library's principal room in the Capitol destroys 35,000 of its 55,000-volume collection, including two-thirds of Jefferson's library.

1853

The American Association for the Advancement of Science advocates "a geographical library" at the Library of Congress, pointing out that "there is not in the United States nor on this continent a single collection of geographical materials that is tolerably complete."

1857

Responsibility for the international exchange of books and documents and for the distribution of public documents, heretofore functions of the Library of Congress, are transferred to the State Department and the Bureau of the Interior, respectively.

1859

The law providing copyright deposits to the Library of Congress and the Smithsonian Institution is repealed.

1865

Librarian of Congress Ainsworth Rand Spofford obtains approval for the expansion of the Library's room in the Capitol and for the reinstatement of the copyright privilege. The Library will receive, for its use, one copy of every copyrighted "book, pamphlet, map, chart, musical composition, print, engraving, or photograph."

1866

The Smithsonian Institution's forty thousand-volume library, strong in scientific works and publications of the learned societies, is transferred to the Library. The Smithsonian retains use of the collection, which also will be available to the public "for purposes of consultation."

1867

The Library becomes the recipient, through the Smithsonian Institution's document exchange system, of public documents published in foreign countries.

1867

The private library of Peter Force is purchased for $100,000 and becomes the foundation of the Library's Americana and incunabula collections.

1869

The emperor of China sends a gift of 933 volumes to the U.S. government, a donation that forms the nucleus of the Library's Chinese collection.

1870

Educator Francis Lieber donates three volumes to the Library. He inscribes them "To the National Library" and explains to Librarian Spofford: "It is not the official name, but I take the liberty. It is the name you have come to."

1870

All U.S. copyright registration and deposit activities are centralized at the Library. Two copies of all copyrighted items are to be sent, along with pre-1870 copyright records and deposits.

1871

Spofford reports to Congress that the increased receipts from the new copyright law "will soon compel the provision of more room for books." As one alternative, he suggests a separate building.

Statesman, innovative printer, and accomplished writer Benjamin Franklin became the first American to achieve an international scientific reputation when Experiments and Observations on Electricity *was published in London in 1751 and was translated shortly thereafter into French. The copy from which this title page is reproduced is in the Rare Book and Special Collections Division.*

1872

Spofford asks officials of twenty-six "leading" American cities to begin sending their city documents to the Library.

1874

The Library Committee authorizes the Librarian to subscribe to at least two newspapers from each state. The newspapers are to reflect different political views.

1882

A law is approved authorizing the donation of the forty thousand-volume private library of Washington physician Joseph Toner to the Library of Congress. Sen. John Sherman of Ohio, on behalf of the Joint Library Committee, notes that the Toner gift represents "the first instance in the history of this government of the free gift of a large and valuable library to the nation."

1882

The U.S. government purchases a portion of the Benjamin Franklin papers; the books and pamphlets are sent to the Library of Congress.

1883

The U.S. government purchases, for the Library of Congress, the papers and maps of comte de Rochambeau.

1884

A gift of 375 volumes from Sultan Abdul-Hamid II of Turkey, acquired through the efforts of Rep. Abram S. Hewitt of New York, establishes the nucleus of the Library's Turkish collection. Each volume is inscribed on the cover, in three languages, "To the national library of the United States of America."

1886

The construction of a separate building for the Library is authorized.

1888

The Library Committee, chaired by Sen. William M. Evarts of New York, notes that little has been done by the government to preserve valuable historical manuscripts, e.g., "Where are the papers, public and private, left by the Presidents of the United States since the time of Monroe?" It recommends the creation of a separate department of manuscripts once the new Library building is opened.

1891

A new copyright law affords protection to works of foreign origin under certain conditions of reciprocal protection and requires deposit of these works in the Library.

1893

Librarian Spofford reports to Congress that it is impossible to provide information about the collections since overcrowding has forced their storage "in sixteen separate halls and storage rooms in the Capitol."

1893

The Library acquires its first motion pictures in the form of *Edison Kinetoscopic Records* deposited for copyright by W. K. L. Dixon.

1895

Approximately seventy tons of unclassified copyright deposits are transferred from the southern crypt under the Capitol to the basement of the nearly completed Library of Congress building.

1897

The Library is reorganized and expanded prior to its move into the new building. The staff is increased from 42 to 108. Separate departments are established to house, serve, and cultivate the periodicals, manuscript, music, graphic arts, and map collections.

1897

The Library's collections are transported across the east plaza of the Capitol to the new Library in horse-drawn wagons. Approximately eight hundred tons of material are moved.

1897

Librarian of Congress John Russell Young asserts one "inflexible" rule regarding the impending reclassification of the Library's collections: "no method of classification should be favored which would disintegrate the general collection."

1898

Librarian Young addresses a letter to U.S. diplomatic and consular representatives around the world, asking them to send research materials that "would add to the sum of human knowledge" to the Library.

1898

The Gardiner Greene Hubbard collection of engravings, the Library's first major collection of fine prints, is donated by his widow, Gertrude M. Hubbard.

1898

Young explains that his paramount duty is "the strengthening of the Library as a collection of books," and that he looks forward to the day when the Library receives, in addition to copyright deposits, increased congressional appropriations for books and "gifts from private sources." He also announces the publication of "bibliographic bulletins" based on the collections, e.g., lists of books for Congress about Cuba and Hawaii.

1899

Librarian of Congress Herbert Putnam informs Congress that the Library's collection is "exceedingly defective" and "may be built up only by incessant solicitation, exchange, and purchase." He recommends $50,000 a year be spent on purchases.

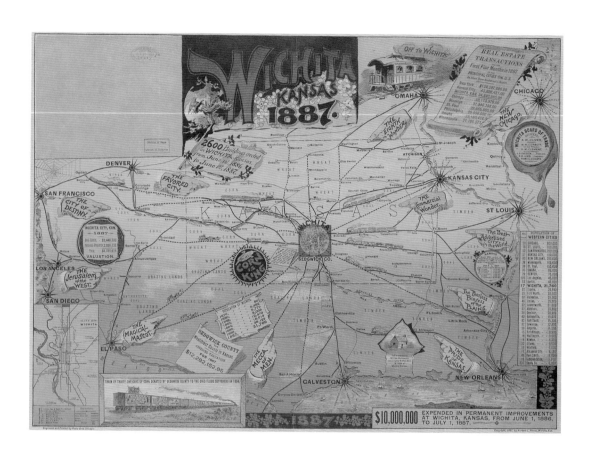

The Library's Geography and Map Division has the largest and most comprehensive cartographic collection in the world—spanning many centuries and including maps in many forms. The colorful map of the southwestern United States, above, showing railroads converging on Wichita, Kansas, from ten large cities around the country, is one of five thousand maps in the division that record the achievements of early North American railroaders. At right is a Landsat map of Salt Lake City, one of nearly seven million worldwide photographic images transferred to the Library by the National Aeronautics and Space Administration, the United States Geological Survey, and the National Oceanic and Atmospheric Administration.

1901

The Library publishes the first new classification schedule based on the re-classification of the collections, *Class E and F: America: History and Geography,* and its first description of a manuscript collection, *A Calendar of Washington Manuscripts in the Library of Congress.*

1901

The Library begins printing, selling, and distributing catalog cards for all books it is cataloging or recataloging.

1901

The cylinder recording of the voice of Kaiser Wilhelm II given to the Library in 1904 became the nucleus of recorded sound collections that now include more than 1.3 million recordings of music and the spoken word from 1890 to the present. These collections include formats that demonstrate the remarkable progressive steps in the history of recording—from wax cylinders to compact discs.

Librarian Putnam reports that the Library of Congress, which is now spending $60,000 a year to purchase research collections, has become the first American library to contain over one million volumes.

1902

Putnam reports that the Library's Orientalia collection of nearly ten thousand volumes appears to be "the largest representation in this country of the literature of the Far East."

1903

A new law authorizes U.S. government agencies to transfer to the Library of Congress "any books, maps, or other material no longer needed for use."

1903

Pres. Theodore Roosevelt issues an executive order that transfers, from the Department of State to the Library of Congress, the records and papers of the Continental Congress and the personal papers of Benjamin Franklin, George Washington, Thomas Jefferson, James Madison, and James Monroe.

1904

A cylinder recording of the voice of Kaiser Wilhelm II is presented to the Library and becomes the first phonograph record in the collections.

1904

Putnam announces a new program: the publication of historical texts from the Library's collections, beginning with the Journals of the Continental Congress and the Records of the Virginia Company.

1904

The Library purchases a four thousand-volume collection of Indica, formerly the library of Albrecht Weber, professor of Sanskrit at the University of Berlin.

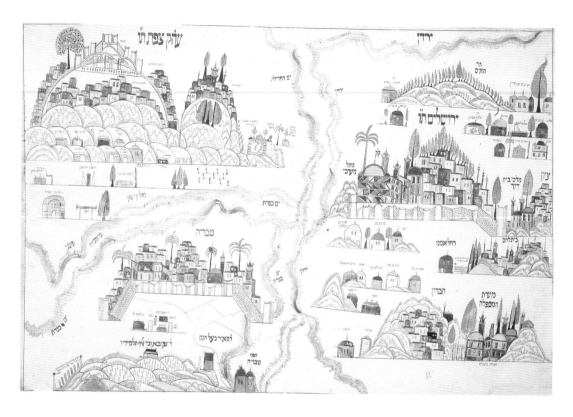

1905

The Library begins a program for copying manuscripts in foreign archives that relate to American history.

1906

Pres. Theodore Roosevelt congratulates Putnam on the purchase of the private library of G. V. Yudin of Siberia, which contains over eighty thousand volumes of Russian literature. The president notes that the acquisition will give the Library of Congress preeminence in this field.

1907

Putnam announces the first large acquisition of Japanese books, nine thousand volumes selected in Japan by Kan-Ichi Asakawa, a Yale University professor.

1907

Putnam recommends to President Roosevelt the construction of a separate archives building to accommodate government administrative records "not appropriate for the collections of the Library."

The Hebraic Section, founded in 1914, has custody of all the Library's materials of research value in Hebrew and related languages. Among its holdings is this charming pastel watercolor wall plaque depicting the holy cities of the Holy Land—Jerusalem, Hebron, Tiberias, and Safed. The plaque was painted in Palestine in the second half of the nineteenth century.

1908

The Library purchases, from Albert Schatz of Rostock, Germany, Mr. Schatz's famous collection of more than twelve thousand early opera librettos.

1909

The copyright law of 1909 authorizes the Librarian of Congress to sell, exchange, or transfer copyright deposits to other government agencies.

1912

A collection of nearly ten thousand volumes and pamphlets of Hebraica, gathered by Ephraim Deinard, is donated to the Library by Jacob H. Schiff of New York City. Putnam calls it a notable foundation which will be expanded "into a significant department embracing all Semitica."

1913

The American Printing House for the Blind begins depositing in the Library of Congress one copy of each embossed book that it produces with federal financial assistance.

1916

Two drafts of Pres. Abraham Lincoln's Gettysburg Address are presented to the U.S. government by the descendants of John Hay and placed in the Library of Congress.

1917

The Library receives the first installment of the gift of the Theodore Roosevelt Papers, the first group of presidential papers received directly from a former president.

1917

Mr. and Mrs. Joseph Pennell present a valuable collection of prints and sketches by James Whistler to the Library, along with a collection of books and research materials about the artist and his era.

1920

More than three hundred original daguerreotype portraits of prominent Americans made between the years 1845 and 1853 by the studio of photographer Mathew B. Brady are transferred to the Library from the U.S. Army War College.

1921

The original copies of the Declaration of Independence and the Constitution of the United States are transferred to the Library from the State Department.

Capítulo 5.º

De como los Mexicanos avisados de
su Dios fuéron á vuscar el Tunal y
el Aguila, y como lo halláron, y del
acuerdo que para el edificio tubiéron

Otro dia de mañana el Sacerdote
Juauhtloquetzqui, cuidadoso de rebelar la re-

1923

Robert Todd Lincoln, son of Pres. Abraham Lincoln, donates his father's papers to the Library.

1925

A new law establishes the Library of Congress Trust Fund Board, enabling the Library to accept gifts and bequests of personal property for the benefit of the Library.

1925

Elizabeth Sprague Coolidge establishes an endowment to aid the Library's Music Division "in the development of the study, composition, and appreciation of music."

1926

James B. Childs, Chief of the Documents Division, visits Germany, Lithuania, Latvia, and Russia "to form new connections" for the acquisition of government publications.

1927

Archer M. Huntington of New York City presents the Library of Congress Trust Fund Board with funds to establish an endowment "for the purchase of books relating to Spanish, Portuguese, and South American arts, crafts, literature, and history."

1928

Putnam establishes an American folk song project in the Music Division to collect and preserve the folk songs and ballads now "endangered by the spread of the radio and phonograph."

1930

Supreme Court Justice Harlan F. Stone testifies before the House Appropriations Subcommittee in support of a larger appropriation for the Law Library. He explains that he and Justice Louis B. Brandeis are both eager for the Library of Congress to develop "a great collection" which will be of service "for all time."

1930

A law is approved authorizing the purchase for $1.5 million of the Vollbehr collection of incunabula, which includes more than three thousand items and one of three perfect vellum copies of the Gutenberg Bible.

The Lessing J. Rosenwald Collection, comprising more than twenty-six hundred rare illustrated books, stands out among the distinguished resources of the Rare Book and Special Collections Division. Among the outstanding selection of works by William Blake in the Rosenwald Collection is the 1794 edition of Europe, A Prophecy, *from which the page above is reproduced. The page reproduced at right is from the fifteenth-century folio edition of Anicius Boethius's great work De Consolatione Philosophiae.

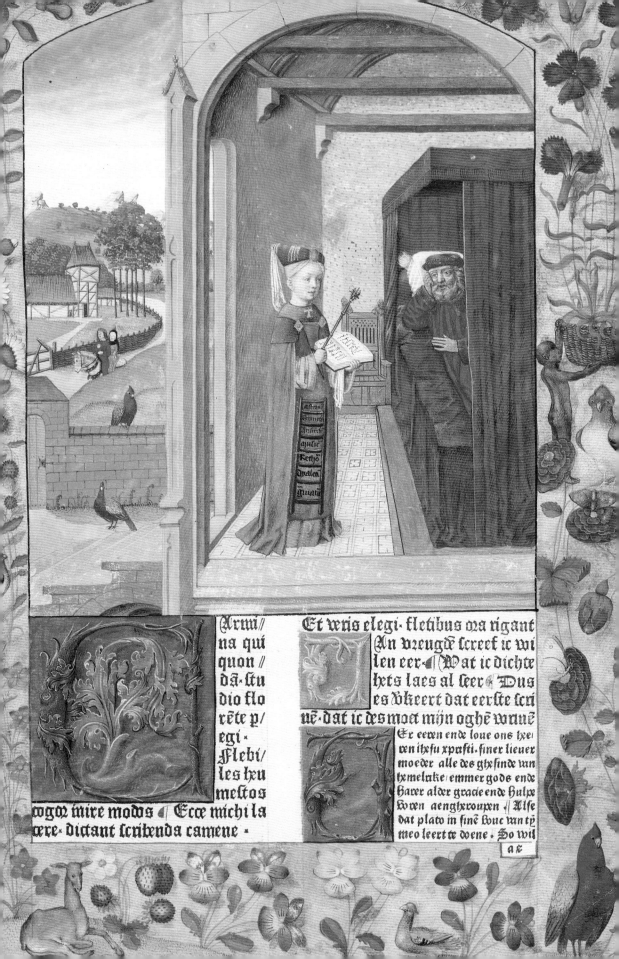

Armi//
na qui
quon//
dā-stu
dio flo
rēte p/
egi·
Flebi/
les heu
mestos
cogor mire modus·｜Ecce michi la
cere·dictant scribenda camene·

Et wris elegi· fletibus ma rigant
An vreugdē screef ic wi
len eer·｜Wat ic dichte
hets laes al seer｜Dus
es vkeert dat eerste scri
uē·dat ic des moot mijn oghē wriuē

Er eewen ende loue ons txe
wen ihxfu xpasti·finer lieuer
moeder alle des ghx sinde van
txmelxke emmer gods ende
Bater alder grace ende hulpe
wren aenghxroupen｜Alse
dat plato in sine bouc van ty
meo leert te doene· So wil

ax

1931

A separate annual appropriation for books "for the use of the adult blind readers of the United States" is approved.

1934

Putnam explains to Congress that the Library of Congress is now the largest library in the world, but he cautions that the methods of counting used by the British Museum Library and the Bibliothèque Nationale "are somewhat different from ours, and it is not safe to undertake comparisons."

1934

The Library becomes the repository for photographs and drawings from the Historic American Buildings Survey.

1936

Gertrude Clarke Whittall establishes an endowment to support the "care and use" of the five Stradavari instruments she has donated to the Library.

1938

Using funds received from the Rockefeller Foundation, the Library establishes a Photoduplication Service for the purpose of "competently supplying distant investigators with microfilm and other photoduplicates of materials otherwise not available for use outside Washington."

1938

The Carnegie Corporation gives the Library a three-year grant for the development of its Indica collection.

1939

The Library's committee on acquisitions, aided by specialists from the academic community, reports serious weaknesses in the Library's collections and recommends that the annual appropriation for book purchases be increased dramatically. Of the forty principal subjects in the Library's classification system, twelve are considered strong, thirteen are adequate, and fifteen are inadequate.

1939

The first gift from the Gershwin family establishes the George and Ira Gershwin Collection.

1940

The Library of Congress Works Projects Administration (WPA) Project begins collecting materials produced by the federal art, music, theatre, and writers' projects and the Historical Records Survey.

1940

Librarian of Congress Archibald MacLeish announces a grant from the Carnegie Corporation to establish a recording laboratory in the Music Division.

1940

Librarian MacLeish begins an administrative reorganization of the Library and presents comprehensive statements of the Library's acquisitions policies (The Canons of Selection) and of its research objectives (The Canons of Service).

1941

MacLeish announces the establishment of the Gertrude Clarke Whittall Foundation Collection of Musical Autographs. The first purchase is a collection of original manuscripts by Beethoven, Brahms, Michael Haydn, Mozart, Schubert, Wagner, and Weber.

1942

Uruguayan poet Emilio Oribe records one of his latest poems at the Library, inaugurating the Archive of Hispanic Literature on Tape.

1942

MacLeish announces a new program for acquiring and preserving American motion pictures.

1943

The Library announces the gift of a "magnificent collection of rare books and manuscripts" from Lessing J. Rosenwald of Jenkintown, Pennsylvania. Over five hundred choice rare books, many of them illustrated, are in the Rosenwald Collection. It includes more than two hundred incunabula.

1943

In connection with its celebration of the bicentennial of Thomas Jefferson's birth, the Library publishes *The Declaration of Independence: The Evolution of a Text,* by Julian P. Boyd. It also begins microfilming Jefferson's papers.

1943

MacLeish announces the purchase of more than nine thousand negative plates and photographs by Arnold Genthe, "a pioneer in the field of photography." He also establishes a new committee "to insure the proper development" of the Library's photographic archive.

1944

The Library assumes custody of the Office of War Information collection of nearly 300,000 photographs, including the "photo-documentation of America" file organized by Roy E. Stryker in the Farm Security Administration from 1936 to 1942.

1945

The Library purchases the personal library of Sheikh Mahmud al-Imam Mansuri of Cairo, which contains over five thousand books and manuscripts and greatly strengthens the Arabic collections.

1945

Under the leadership of Librarian of Congress Luther H. Evans, the Library establishes a "mission in Europe" to obtain "multiple copies of European publications for the war period" for distribution to American libraries and research institutions. A cooperative acquisitions program for European wartime publications is established.

1946

Edith Bolling Wilson, widow of the former president, donates the nine thousand-volume personal library of Woodrow Wilson to the Library.

1949

The papers of Orville and Wilbur Wright, thirty thousand items in sixty-eight boxes and including 303 glass-plate negatives documenting their successes and failures with the new flying machines, are donated to the Library.

1950

Chicago businessman Alfred Whital Stern donates "the most extensive collection of Lincoln literature ever assembled by a private individual" to the Library.

1952

Lessing J. Rosenwald formally presents to the Library, as a gift to the nation, the Giant Bible of Mainz—a magnificent illuminated manuscript Bible written in Mainz, Germany, between April 4, 1452, and July 9, 1453.

In 1943, the Library purchased the materials remaining in the studio of photographer Arnold Genthe (1869–1943) at the time of his death. This collection, approximately ten thousand negatives and eighty-seven hundred contact and enlargement prints, is the largest single assemblage of Genthe's work. Among Genthe's portraits of prominent artists and writers is this exceptional photograph of author Pearl Buck, who won the 1938 Nobel Prize in Literature.

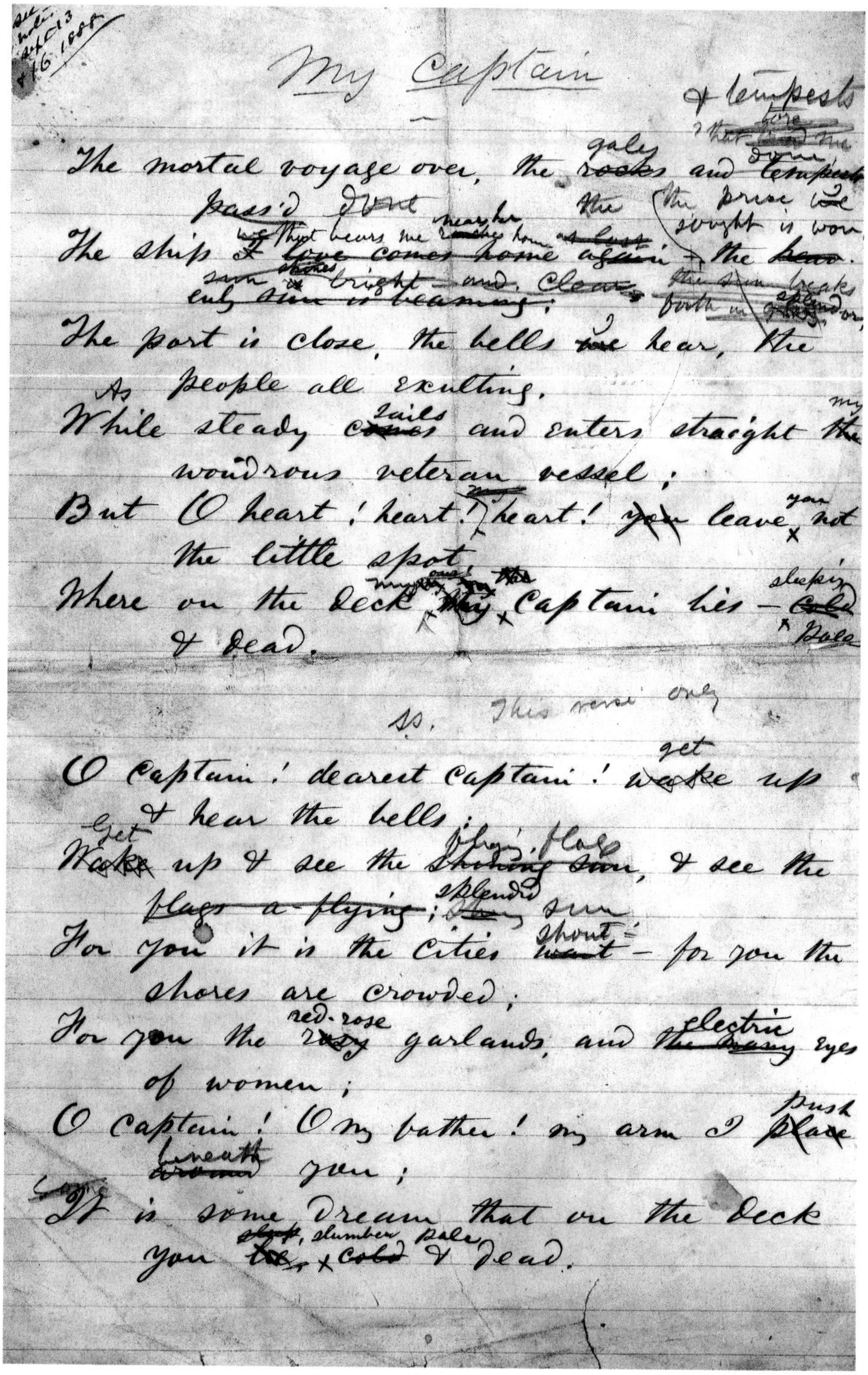

My Captain

& tempests

The mortal voyage over, the ~~rocks~~ gales and ~~tempests~~
pass'd ~~d'ont~~
The ship ~~that bears me~~ ~~comes home again~~ ~~the~~ the prize we
~~only sun is beaming;~~ bright and clear ~~the sun breaks
forth in splendor~~

The port is close, the bells we hear, the
As people all exulting,
While steady ~~comes~~ sails and enters straight the my
wondrous veteran vessel;
But O heart! heart! heart! ~~you~~ leave you not
the little spot,
Where on the deck ~~My~~ Captain lies — sleeping
& dead.

ss. This were only

O Captain! dearest Captain! ~~wake~~ get up
& hear the bells;
Get
~~Wake~~ up & see the ~~shining sun~~, flag & see the
~~flags a-flying~~; splendid sun
For you it is the cities ~~want~~ shout — for you the
shores are crowded;
For you the red-rose ~~rosy~~ garlands, and ~~the many~~ electric eyes
of women;
O Captain! O my father! my arm I ~~place~~ push
~~beneath~~ you;
It is some Dream that on the deck
you ~~lie~~ slumber pale cold & dead.

70

The Feinberg-Whitman Collection in the Manuscript Division, and the Walt Whitman Collection in the Rare Book and Special Collections Division constitute the largest group of materials relating to American poet Walt Whitman ever assembled. At left is a page from a draft of "O Captain! My Captain!" The photograph of Whitman, above, was taken in his sitting-room in Camden, N.J., where he lived the last eight years of his life.

1952

The Joint Committee on the Library directs Librarian Evans to transfer the Declaration of Independence and the Constitution of the United States to the National Archives.

1952

The Library receives the first installment of the Sigmund Freud papers.

1952

The Library publishes the first of five volumes of a definitive catalog of Thomas Jefferson's personal library "as it was at the time of its sale to the Nation in 1815." E. Millicent Sowerby is the compiler.

1954

The Library receives, as a gift, the Brady-Handy photographic collection, which contains over 3,000 negatives made by Civil War photographer Mathew B. Brady and several thousand plates made by his nephew, Levin C. Handy. The collection is donated by L. C. Handy's daughters.

1957

Defending an increase in the Library's budget, Congressman Clarence Cannon of Missouri, chairman of the House Committee on Appropriations, states: "The Library of Congress is the greatest library in the world. It is the visible, irrefutable evidence of the academic and intellectual achievement of the American people. Let no action . . . retard the continued growth and development of this national institution."

1958

Librarian of Congress L. Quincy Mumford establishes a committee on mechanical information retrieval to study "the problem of applying machine methods to the control of the Library's general collections."

1958

Public Law 83–480 (P.L. 480) authorizes the Library to use U.S.-owned foreign currencies to acquire books, periodicals, and other materials for other libraries and research centers in the United States.

1959
A grant from the Carnegie Corporation supports the establishment of an Africana section, enabling the Library "to exploit more fully its outstanding collection of Africana."

1961
The Library's first P.L. 480 acquisitions offices open in New Delhi and Cairo.

1963
The Library establishes a Children's Literature Center, "to serve those who serve children."

1964
The Library receives the first installment of the gift of the records of the National Association for the Advancement of Colored People (NAACP), an archive of more than one million items.

1966
Title IIC of the Higher Education Act of 1965 authorizes the Library to acquire current library materials and provide cataloging information for these materials to libraries around the nation.

1966
The Library's first overseas acquisitions office in the new National Program for Acquisitions and Cataloging opens in London.

1968
The Library and the American Film Institute conclude a cooperative agreement for the further development of the Library's national motion picture collection.

1969
The Library announces the acquisition of the Charles E. Feinberg collection of Walt Whitman manuscripts, letters, books, and memorabilia, which contains more than twenty thousand items.

1969
Antiquarian bookdealer Hans P. Kraus donates to the Library a notable collection of 162 manuscripts relating to the history and culture of Spanish America in the colonial period.

1975
The papers of Alexander Graham Bell and the Bell family papers are donated to the Library.

1976
President Ford signs Public Law 94–201, the American Folklife Preservation Act, which establishes within the Library the American Folklife Center "to preserve and present American folklife."

1976
The Library receives the gift of the Erwin Swann Collection of American and European caricature drawings from the nineteenth and twentieth centuries.

1977
President Carter signs Public Law 95–129, which establishes a Center for the Book in the Library of Congress to "stimulate public interest and research in the role of the book in the diffusion of knowledge."

1978
The Library receives the NBC Radio Collection of approximately 175,000 transcription discs covering eighty thousand hours of radio programming from 1926 to 1970.

1979
The Library acquires a collection of papers, workbooks, and early experimental recordings of Emile Berliner, who invented disc recording in 1888.

1984
The acquisition by purchase of two large printed globes by the seventeenth-century master Father Vincenzo Coronelli, dated 1688–93, makes the Library's collection of Coronelli's maps and globes virtually complete.

1985
The original drawings for the Vietnam Memorial competition, including Maya Lin's winning design, are acquired by the Library.

1988
The Moldenhauer collection of autograph music manuscripts, letters, and documents, one of the most significant collections of primary source materials in music ever assembled, is donated to the Library, establishing the Hans Moldenhauer Archives.

1988

President Bush signs Public Law 100–446, the National Film Preservation Act of 1988, which requires the Library to choose and preserve up to twenty-five "culturally, historically, or aesthetically significant" films in a National Film Registry each year.

1988

The Library establishes a machine-readable collections reading room to serve materials in machine-readable formats, including microcomputer software programs and information or data files on microcomputer, compact, and video discs.

1989

The Library acquires the Charles and Ray Eames collection of design, which includes more than 700,000 pieces, including papers, drawings, photographs and transparencies, graphics, and motion pictures.

1990

The American Memory Project is established to begin sharing portions of the Library's Americana collections in electronic form.

1991

LC Direct is inaugurated, offering state library agencies online access to the Library's bibliographic, subject, and name authority cards.

1992

The Library acquires the Irving Berlin collection of more 750,000 items, including the musical scores of many of Berlin's most popular compositions.

1992

The 100 millionth item is added to the Library's collections.

The Alexander Graham Bell Family Collection documents a great American inventor. Bell's father, Alexander Melville Bell, developed the physiological alphabet below. At right, Alexander Graham Bell, his wife and son, attend the 1907 opening of Bell's tetrahedral tower.

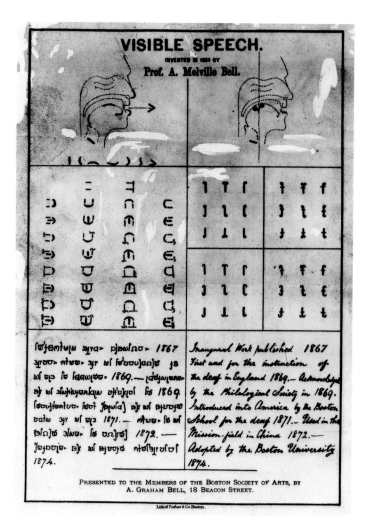

The Buildings

THE LIBRARY OF CONGRESS IN THE CAPITOL, 1800–1897

A stairway in the Great Hall of the Library of Congress, Thomas Jefferson Building, which was designed to demonstrate America's love of learning, science, work, and culture. Previous pages: Neptune, his son Triton, and various sea nymphs, as realized by sculptor Roland Hinton Perry, glow under artificial light in this nighttime photograph of the Court of Neptune Fountain in front of the Jefferson Building.

The law creating the Library of Congress, approved on April 24, 1800, called for its books to be housed in "a suitable apartment" in the Capitol. In 1800 only the north wing of the Capitol was finished. The books brought by Congress from Philadelphia and the new books acquired for the Library were placed in the office of the Clerk of the Senate. During 1801, a temporary structure was built for the use of the House of Representatives, and the act of January 26, 1802, which established the rules and procedures "concerning the Library for the use of both Houses of Congress," provided for the move of the Library into the room in the north wing formerly occupied by the House. Here the Library remained until December 1805.

The Library of Congress occupied various spaces in the Capitol building between 1806 and August 24, 1814, when the British burned the Capitol and the Library. On January 30, 1815, Thomas Jefferson's library was purchased by Congress to "recommence" its library, and a law approved on March 3, 1815, authorized the preparation of "a proper apartment" for the books. Blodget's Hotel at 7th and E Streets was serving as the temporary Capitol, and a room on its third floor became the new location of the Library of Congress. Here Jefferson's books were received and organized by Librarian of Congress George Watterston. On February 18, 1817, Library Committee chairman

Eligius Fromentin, a senator from Louisiana, introduced a resolution advocating a separate building for the Library, but it failed. In late 1818, however, funds were appropriated to move the Library back into the Capitol.

The new quarters in the attic story of the Capitol's north wing proved inadequate. In January 1818 Charles Bulfinch became Architect of the Capitol and he soon developed plans for a spacious library room in the center of the west front of the Capitol. The new room, which measured 90 feet in length and 30 feet wide, was occupied on August 17, 1824. On December 22, 1825, a fire started by a candle left burning in the gallery was controlled before it could cause serious damage. Investigations into fireproofing the room concluded that the expense would be too great. In 1832 a separate "apartment" was established for the law collection.

On Christmas Eve, 1851, the Library of Congress suffered a disastrous fire. Approximately thirty-five thousand of its fifty-five thousand volumes were destroyed in the flames, which were caused by a faulty chimney flue. Architect of the Capitol Thomas U. Walter presented a plan, approved by Congress, to repair and enlarge the Library room using fireproof materials throughout. The elegantly restored Library room was opened on August 23, 1853. Called by the press the "largest iron room in the world," it was encircled by galleries and filled the west central front of the Capitol. A month be-

This drawing of the old Congressional Reading Room by W. Bengough appeared in Harper's Weekly on February 27, 1897. Librarian of Congress Ainsworth Rand Spofford is depicted on the far right, emerging from his desk area with a book for a reader. The man on the left holding the lamp is David Hutcheson, Assistant Librarian.

fore the opening, Pres. Franklin Pierce inspected the new Library in the company of British scientist Sir Charles Lyell, who pronounced it "the most beautiful room in the world."

In 1865, Librarian of Congress Ainsworth Rand Spofford obtained approval for expanding the Library by adding two new fireproof wings. The copyright law of 1870 brought two copies of all copyrighted items to the Library, however, and it immediately became apparent to Librarian Spofford that the Library would soon run out of space. He suggested a separate building and, in 1872, presented a plan to Congress for such a structure. In 1875, he reported to Congress that the Library had exhausted all shelf space and that "books are now, from sheer force of necessity, being piled on the floor in all directions." Unless Congress took quick action on the question of a separate building, he noted, its Librarian would soon be placed "in the unhappy predicament of presiding over the greatest chaos in America."

THE JEFFERSON BUILDING

The first separate Library of Congress Building, the Jefferson Building, was suggested by Librarian of Congress Ainsworth Rand Spofford in 1871, authorized in 1886, and completed in 1897. When its doors were opened to the public on November 1, 1897, it represented an unparalleled national achievement: its 23-carat gold-plated dome capped the "largest, costliest, and safest" library building in the world. Its elaborately decorated facade and interior, for which more than forty American painters and sculptors produced works of art, were designed to demonstrate that the United States could surpass European libraries in grandeur and devotion to classical culture. A contemporary guidebook boasted: "America is justly proud of this gorgeous and palatial monument to its National sympathy and appreciation of Literature, Science, and Art. It has been designed and executed entirely by American art and American labor (and is) a fitting tribute for the great thoughts of generations past, present, and to be." This new national Temple of the Arts immediately met with overwhelming approval from the American public.

Known as the Library of Congress (or Main) Building until it was named for Thomas Jefferson, the Library's principal founder, in 1980, the structure was built specifically to serve as the American national library, and its architecture and decoration express and enhance that purpose. A national library for the United States was the dream and goal of Librarian Spofford; the new building was a crucial step in his achievement. It was a functional, state-of-the-art structure as well as a Temple of the Arts, using the latest technology throughout.

The early years of planning and construction were filled with controversy and delay. After two design competitions and a decade of debate about design and location, in 1886 Congress finally chose an Italian Renaissance plan submitted by Washington architects John L. Smithmeyer and Paul J. Pelz. Structurally the architects followed the basic idea proposed by Librarian Spofford: a circular, domed reading room at the Library's center, surrounded by ample space for the Library's various departments. In the final Smithmeyer & Pelz plan the reading room was enclosed by rectangular exterior walls, which divided the open space into four courtyards.

Disputes continued after the building was authorized in 1886. Responsibility for clearing the site was unclear (several buildings had to be razed) and Capitol landscape architect Frederick Law Olmsted protested the building's location, which shut out "the whole view of the Capitol building from Pennsylvania Avenue—the main approach from Capitol hill." Another controversy, this one about the selection of the proper cement for the foundation, proved to be architect Smithmeyer's undoing, and he was dismissed in 1888. The building's construction was placed under the direction of Brig. Gen. Thomas Lincoln Casey, Chief of the U.S. Army Corps of Engineers. Casey and his Superintendent of Construction, civil engineer Bernard R. Green, had successfully completed the construction of the Washington Monument and the State, War, and Navy (now the Old Executive Office) Building and were trusted by the Congress. The cornerstone was laid in 1890. Paul Pelz, who replaced Smithmeyer as architect in 1888, was himself dismissed in 1892 and replaced by architect Edward Pearce Casey, General Casey's son, who supervised most of the interior decoration.

Known primarily for their ability to keep construction costs to a minimum, General Casey and Bernard Green were infused with a nationalism which complemented Spofford's national library aspirations. They viewed the interior art work as a necessary component in carrying out the building's monumental design and purpose. They also wanted to give American artists an opportunity to display their talents, and employed no less than forty-two American sculptors and painters "to fully and consistently carry out the monumental design and purpose of the building." In a report to Congress in 1896, Superintendent Green stated that the total cost of the mural and decorative

In 1986 work began on a massive renovation of the Thomas Jefferson Building as it approached its one hundredth birthday in 1997. Above, the heart of that building, the Main Reading Room, is shown before renovation. The photograph at right shows the renovation, undertaken in stages, painstakingly in progress. The renovated Main Reading Room reopened in 1991.

painting, the sculpture, and the three massive bronze doors at the main entrance (representing Tradition, Writing, and Printing), was $364,000. In addition, Hinton Perry's fifty-foot-wide fountain in front of the building, which depicts a scene in the court of Neptune, cost $22,000. The price of gilding the dome, including the flame of the Torch of Learning at its apex, was $3,800. Yet, the building was still completed for $200,000 less than the total congressional authorization of approximately $6,500,000.

Since 1897, the gilded copper dome has been replaced, and three of the four interior courtyards of the Jefferson Building have been filled. The east courtyards have become bookstacks: the southeast bookstack was completed in 1910, the northeast in 1927. The Coolidge Auditorium, opened in 1925, and the Whittall Pavilion, opened in 1939, occupy the northwest courtyard. The east side of the Jefferson Building was extended in the early 1930s, providing new quarters for the Rare Book Room when construction was completed in 1934. The Main Reading Room was closed for renovation in 1964–65. In 1984, Congress appropriated $81.5 million for the renovation and restoration of the Jefferson and Adams buildings. Work started in 1986 and is scheduled for completion in 1995.

The Jefferson Building is a heroic setting for a national institution. Today it is generally recognized as a unique blending of art and architecture, a structure that celebrates the universality of knowledge and symbolizes American turn-of-the-century optimism. The elaborate embellishment of its interior is worth careful attention, for few structures represent human thought and aspiration in such dramatic fashion.

The second Library building, originally called the Annex Building, was renamed for man of letters and second president of the United States John Adams in 1980. The building's bronze doors, pictured at left, are decorated with representations, by sculptor Lee Lawrie, of historical figures credited with giving the art of writing to their people since ancient times.

THE ADAMS BUILDING

In 1928, at the urging of Librarian of Congress Herbert Putnam, Congress authorized the purchase of land directly east of the Library's Main Building for the construction of an Annex Building. In 1930, $6,500,000 was appropriated for its construction, for a tunnel connecting it to the Main Building, and for certain changes in the east front of the Main Building, including the construction of the Rare Book Room. An additional appropriation in 1935 brought the total provision of funds to over $8 million. The simple classical structure was intended, essentially, as a functional and efficient bookstack "encircled with work spaces." It was designed by the Washington architectural firm of Pierson & Wilson, with Alexander Buel Trowbridge as consulting architect. The contract stipulated completion by June 24, 1938, but the building was not ready for occupancy until December 2, 1938. The move of the Card Division started on December 12, and it opened its doors for business to the public in the new building on January 3, 1939.

On April 13, 1976, in a ceremony at the Jefferson Memorial marking the birthday of Thomas Jefferson, President Ford signed into law the act to change the name of the Library of Congress Annex Building to the Library of Congress Thomas Jefferson Building. In 1980, the structure acquired its present name, which honors John Adams, the man of letters and president of the United States who in 1800 approved the law establishing the Library of Congress.

The dignified exterior of the Adams Building is faced with white Georgia marble. Its twelve tiers of stacks provide about thirteen acres of shelf space and shelf capacity for about ten million books.

Today, the building's decorative style, which contains elements of "Art Deco" inspired by the Exposition des Arts Décoratifs held in Paris in 1925, is widely admired. The history of the written word is depicted in sculptured figures by Lee Lawrie on the bronze doors at the west (Second Street) and east (Third Street) entrances. Decorative features in the first floor lobbies and corridors and in the fifth floor lobbies and reading rooms are worth special note.

On the fifth floor, the north reading room is decorated by murals by artist Ezra Winter that illustrate the characters in Geoffrey Chaucer's *Canterbury Tales*.

Four murals by Ezra Winter decorate the South Reading Room. The theme is drawn from the quotations from Thomas Jefferson's writings which are inscribed in the murals and reflect Jefferson's thoughts on Freedom, Labor, the

The North Reading Room on the fifth floor of the Adams Building, pictured above, holds a reference collection focused primarily on business and economics, political science, education, and sociology. Among its most prominent decorative elements are near-life-size paintings of all of Chaucer's Canterbury pilgrims by artist Ezra Winter.

The northern lunette in the South Reading Room of the Adams Building dedicates the room to Thomas Jefferson. Murals by Ezra Winter and devoted to Jefferson decorate all the reading room's walls, accompanied by side panels containing quotations from Jefferson's writings which demonstrate the breadth of his interests and his philosophy.

Living Generation, Education, and Democratic Government. The characters and costumes depicted are those of Jefferson's time. A portrait of Jefferson with his residence, Monticello, in the background is in a lunette over the reference desk at the north end of the room.

On the left half of the panel on the east wall, Jefferson's view on Freedom:

THE GROUND OF LIBERTY IS TO BE GAINED BY INCHES. WE MUST BE CONTENTED TO SECURE WHAT WE CAN GET FROM TIME TO TIME AND ETERNALLY PRESS FORWARD FOR WHAT IS YET TO GET. IT TAKES TIME TO PERSUADE MEN TO DO EVEN WHAT IS FOR THEIR OWN GOOD.

Jefferson to Rev. Charles Clay, January 27, 1790

His views on Labor also are on the east wall:

THOSE WHO LABOR IN THE EARTH ARE THE CHOSEN PEOPLE OF GOD, IF HE EVER HAD A CHOSEN PEOPLE, WHOSE BREASTS HE HAS MADE THE PECULIAR DEPOSITS FOR SUBSTANTIAL AND GENUINE VIRTUE. IT IS THE FOCUS IN WHICH HE KEEPS ALIVE THAT SACRED FIRE WHICH OTHERWISE MIGHT ESCAPE FROM THE EARTH.

From Notes on Virginia, *1782*

On the south wall, the panel over the clock contains a quotation about the Living Generation:

THE EARTH BELONGS ALWAYS TO THE LIVING GENERATION. THEY MAY MANAGE IT THEN, AND WHAT PROCEEDS FROM IT, AS THEY PLEASE DURING THEIR USUFRUCT. THEY ARE MASTERS TOO OF THEIR OWN PERSONS, AND CONSEQUENTLY MAY GOVERN THEM AS THEY PLEASE.

Jefferson to James Madison, September 6, 1789

On the left half of the panel on the west wall, Jefferson's view of Education is illustrated by the quotation:

EDUCATE AND INFORM THE MASS OF THE PEOPLE. ENABLE THEM TO SEE THAT IT IS THEIR INTEREST TO PRESERVE PEACE AND ORDER, AND THEY WILL PRESERVE THEM. ENLIGHTEN THE PEOPLE GENERALLY, AND TYRANNY AND OPPRESSION OF THE BODY AND MIND WILL VANISH LIKE EVIL SPIRITS AT THE DAWN OF DAY.

Jefferson to James Madison, December 20, 1787 (first two sentences)
Jefferson to P. S. Dupont de Nemours, April 24, 1816 (last sentence)

Jefferson's views on Democratic Government, also on the west wall, are illustrated by the quotation:

THE PEOPLE OF EVERY COUNTRY ARE THE ONLY SAFE GUARDIANS OF THEIR OWN RIGHTS, AND ARE THE ONLY INSTRUMENTS WHICH CAN BE USED FOR THEIR DESTRUCTION. IT IS AN AXIOM IN MY MIND THAT OUR LIBERTY CAN NEVER BE SAFE BUT IN THE HANDS OF THE PEOPLE THEMSELVES, THAT, TOO, OF THE PEOPLE WITH A CERTAIN DEGREE OF INSTRUCTION.

Jefferson to John Wyche, May 19, 1809 (first sentence)
Jefferson to George Washington, January 4, 1786 (second sentence)

The James Madison Memorial Building is the Library's newest building and the nation's official memorial to Madison—fourth president of the United States, and "Father of the United States Constitution." This statue by Walter Hancock is the most prominent feature in the memorial hall on the first floor of the building. Eight quotes from Madison's writings are on the surrounding walls.

THE JAMES MADISON MEMORIAL BUILDING

In 1957, Librarian of Congress L. Quincy Mumford initiated studies for a third Library building. Congress appropriated planning funds for that structure, today's James Madison Memorial Building, in 1960 and construction was authorized in 1965. The cornerstone was laid in 1974 and Pres. Ronald Reagan participated in dedication ceremonies on November 20, 1981, when the building was completed. The building serves both as the Library's third major structure and as this nation's official memorial to James Madi-

son, the "father" of the Constitution and the Bill of Rights and the fourth president of the United States.

That a major Library of Congress building should also become a memorial to James Madison is fitting, for the institution's debt to him is considerable. In 1783, as a member of the Continental Congress, Madison became the first sponsor of the idea of a library for Congress by proposing a list of books that would be useful to legislators, an effort that preceded by seventeen years the establishment of the Library of Congress. In 1815, Madison was president of the United States and a keen observer when the library of his close personal friend and collaborator, Thomas Jefferson, became the foundation of a renewed Library of Congress. Like Jefferson, he was a man of books and an enlightened statesman who believed the power of knowledge was essential for individual liberty and democratic government.

The Madison Building, left, houses the Librarian's Office, the Copyright Office, the Congressional Research Service, the Law Library, and a variety of special collections. The building's sixth floor cafeteria and dining rooms are available to tourists as well as congressional staff, its meeting rooms are often the scenes of free poetry readings and panel discussions, and its exhibition areas are constantly filled with treasures from the Library's collections.

Two quotations from Madison about knowledge, liberty, and learning, are located on each side of the main entrance of the Madison Building on Independence Avenue.

On the left side of the main entrance:

KNOWLEDGE WILL FOREVER GOVERN IGNORANCE; AND A PEOPLE WHO MEAN TO BE THEIR OWN GOVERNOURS, MUST ARM THEMSELVES WITH THE POWER WHICH KNOWLEDGE GIVES.

Madison to W. T. Barry, August 4, 1822

On the right side of the entrance:

WHAT SPECTACLE CAN BE MORE EDIFYING OR MORE SEASONABLE, THAN THAT OF LIBERTY AND LEARNING, EACH LEANING ON THE OTHER FOR THEIR MUTUAL AND SUREST SUPPORT?

Madison to W. T. Barry, August 4, 1822

Modern in style, the Madison Building was designed by the firm of DeWitt, Poor, and Shelton, Associated Architects. It is one of the three largest public buildings in the Washington, D.C., area (the others are the Pentagon and the F.B.I. Building), and contains 2,100,000 square feet with 1,500,000 square feet of assignable space. It houses administrative offices, including the Office of the Librarian, as well as the Copyright Office, the Congressional Research Service, and the Law Library. The building also holds the Library's map, manuscript, music, motion picture, newspaper, and graphic arts collections, and eight of the Library's reading rooms.

Over the main entrance is a four-story relief in bronze, "Falling Books," by Frank Eliscu. Off the entrance hall to the immediate left is the James Madison Memorial Hall, which has eight quotations from Madison on its walls. A heroic statue by Walter Hancock in the center portrays Madison as a young man in his thirties, holding in his right hand volume 83 of the *Encyclopédie Méthodique,* which was published in Paris between 1782–1832. At the end of the entrance hall, above the doorways to the Manuscript Reading Room and the Manuscript Division office, are a pair of bronze medallions by Robert Alexander Weinmann. The one on the left shows the profile of Madison and the one on the right depicts Madison at work.

Librarians of Congress

The office of Librarian of Congress, like the Library of Congress itself, has been shaped by tradition, politics, and strong personalities. Although the Library of Congress was established in 1800, the office of Librarian was not created until 1802. This 1802 law stipulated that the Librarian of Congress was to be appointed by the president—not by the Congress. In fact, Congress had no formal role in the appointment process until 1897, when the Senate gained the privilege of confirming the president's selection. No special qualifications are prescribed by law for the job of Librarian of Congress. Nor is a term of office specified, even though in the twentieth century the precedent seems to have been established that a Librarian of Congress is appointed for life. The office of the Librarian of Congress carried little formal authority until 1897, when the same law that gave the Senate the power to approve a president's nomination of the Librarian gave the Librarian sole responsibility for making the institution's rules and regulations and appointing its staff.

JOHN J. BECKLEY (1802–1807)

On January 29, 1802, Pres. Thomas Jefferson appointed the Clerk of the House of Representatives, his political ally John J. Beckley, to serve concurrently as the first Librarian of Congress. Beckley was born in England on August 4, 1757, and was sent to Virginia eleven years later to work as a scribe for a mercantile firm. He was the first Clerk of the House of Representatives, as well as the first Librarian of Congress. His salary as Librarian could not exceed two dollars a day. John Beckley died on April 8, 1807. His son Alfred inherited a large tract of unsettled land in what today is West Virginia and built the first house in a village that became the city of Beckley, named so by Alfred to honor his father.

PATRICK MAGRUDER (1807–1815)

After Beckley's death, President Jefferson considered separating the offices of Clerk of the House of Representatives and Librarian of Congress, but he did not. On November 7, 1807, Jefferson appointed Patrick Magruder, a Washington newspaperman and former congressman who had been named clerk of the House ten days earlier, to serve concurrently as Librarian of Congress. Magruder was born in 1768 at "Locust Grove," the family estate in Montgomery County, Maryland. On August 24, 1814, the British captured Washington and burned the U.S. Capitol, including the Library of Congress, which was in the Capitol's north wing. After a congressional investigation about the loss of the Library and the use of Library funds, on January 28, 1815, Magruder resigned his position of Clerk of the House of Representatives and by inference, the office of Librarian of Congress. Patrick Magruder died on December 24, 1819.

GEORGE WATTERSTON (1815–1829)

On March 21, 1815, Pres. James Madison appointed George Watterston as the new Librarian of Congress. A local novelist and journalist, Watterston was the first Librarian who was not also the Clerk of the House of Representatives. Watterston, Washington's leading man of letters, was the Librarian of Congress who received Jefferson's library in 1815 and adopted Jefferson's basic classification scheme as the Library's own. A partisan Whig, his librarianship came to an abrupt end on May 28, 1829, when newly elected Pres. Andrew Jackson replaced him with a Librarian who was a Democrat. Watterston was born on October 23, 1783, on a ship in New York harbor; he died in Washington on February 4, 1854.

JOHN SILVA MEEHAN (1829–1861)

On May 28, 1829, Pres. Andrew Jackson appointed a fellow Democrat, local printer and publisher John Silva Meehan, as Librarian of Congress. In early March 1861, Library Committee chairman James A. Pearce of Maryland informed newly elected Pres. Abraham Lincoln that for the past fifteen years the president "has always deferred to the wishes of Congress" regarding the appointment of the Librarian, and that the Library Committee wished to retain Librarian Meehan. However, Lincoln replaced Meehan with a political supporter, John G. Stephenson, two months later. In length of service as Librarian, Meehan ranks only behind Herbert Putnam and Ainsworth Rand Spofford. John Silva Meehan was born in New York City on February 6, 1790, and died in Washington in his residence on Capitol Hill, not far from the Library of Congress, on April 24, 1863.

JOHN G. STEPHENSON (1861–1864)

On May 24, 1861, President Lincoln rewarded a political supporter, John G. Stephenson, a physician from Terre Haute, Indiana, with the job of Librarian of Congress. In September 1861, Stephenson named an ardent bookman with Republican credentials, Ainsworth Rand Spofford, as Assistant Librarian. Stephenson resigned on December 22, 1864, to be effective December 31, 1864. John G. Stephenson was born in Lancaster, New Hampshire, on March 1, 1828, and died on November 12, 1883, in Washington, D.C. He is buried in an unmarked grave in Washington's Congressional Cemetery.

AINSWORTH RAND SPOFFORD
(1864–1897)

When it became apparent that Librarian Stephenson was going to resign, Assistant Librarian Spofford began to gather political endorsements for the job, and on December 31, 1864, President Lincoln appointed Ainsworth Rand Spofford to be the sixth Librarian of Congress. In 1896, on the eve of the move into the Library's first separate building, the leaders of the American Library Association made it clear that they hoped the 71-year-old Spofford would step aside in favor of a younger and more progressive professional library administrator. On June 30, 1897, Pres. William McKinley nominated John Russell Young to be Librarian of Congress; the next day, Young named Spofford as Chief Assistant Librarian, an important job which Spofford held until his death. Ainsworth Rand Spofford was born in Gilmanton, New Hampshire, on September 12, 1825; he died on August 11, 1908, and is buried in Rock Creek Cemetery, Washington, D.C.

JOHN RUSSELL YOUNG
(1897–1899)

Pres. William McKinley appointed a friend and fellow Republican, journalist and former diplomat John Russell Young, as Librarian of Congress on June 30, 1897. The reorganization of the Library approved on February 19, 1897, strengthened the office of the Librarian and required Senate confirmation of the president's choice as Librarian; on June 30, Young became the first Librarian of Congress to be so confirmed. In making his appointments to a greatly expanded Library of Congress and in his devotion to the Library as a "true library of research," he established a new professionalism at the Library. After Young, who died in office on January 17, 1899, the personal qualifications of potential Librarians of Congress became more important than political considerations. John Russell Young was born in Ireland on November 20, 1840. He spent most of his life in Philadelphia.

HERBERT PUTNAM (1899–1939)

John Russell Young's death after only a year and a half in office gave President McKinley a second opportunity to appoint a Librarian of Congress. At the urging of the American Library Association, on March 13, 1899, he named Herbert Putnam, librarian of the Boston Public Library and ALA president-elect. Putnam, who took the oath of office on April 5, was confirmed by the Senate, without debate, on December 12, 1899. He was the first experienced librarian to direct the Library of Congress, and made American libraries a new and important constituency for the Library of Congress. In 1938, Putnam informed Pres. Franklin D. Roosevelt that he was ready to retire. The position of Librarian Emeritus was created on June 20, 1938, but the president asked him to stay on until a successor could be found. Putnam assumed the office of Librarian Emeritus on October 1, 1939, the day before his successor assumed his duties. Herbert Putnam was born on September 20, 1861, in the home of his parents in New York City. He died on August 14, 1955, in Woods Hole, Massachusetts.

ARCHIBALD MACLEISH (1939–1944)

On May 11, 1939, Supreme Court Justice Felix Frankfurter endorsed Pres. Franklin D. Roosevelt's suggestion that poet and writer Archibald MacLeish, "a scholarly man of letters," would make a good Librarian of Congress. Frankfurter felt MacLeish was an appropriate choice because the Library of Congress "is not merely a library." The president nominated MacLeish on June 7. The Senate held hearings on June 13 and 19; opponents of the nomination charged MacLeish with pro-Communist leanings. On June 18, the American Library Association adopted a resolution opposing the nomination because MacLeish was not a library administrator. The Senate confirmed the nomination on June 29 by a vote of 63 to 8, with 25 not voting. On July 10, at the post office in Conway, Massachusetts, MacLeish took the oath of office as the ninth Librarian of Congress. He assumed his duties on October 2, 1939. He resigned on December 19, 1944, to become assistant secretary of state. Archibald MacLeish was born on May 7, 1892, in Glencoe, Illinois. He died in Boston, Massachusetts on April 20, 1982.

LUTHER H. EVANS (1945–1953)

President Roosevelt died on April 12, 1945, without having nominated a successor to MacLeish. On June 18, 1945, Pres. Harry Truman nominated Chief Assistant Librarian of Congress Luther H. Evans to be Librarian of Congress. Evans was a political scientist but also an experienced library administrator who was acceptable to the American Library Association. The Senate held hearings on June 18, and the nominee was confirmed, without objection, on June 29. He took the oath of office on June 30, 1945. On July 1, 1953, Evans was elected the third director-general of UNESCO and submitted his resignation as Librarian of Congress, effective July 5, to Pres. Dwight D. Eisenhower. Luther Evans was born on October 13, 1902, at his grandmother's farm near Sayersville, Bastrop County, Texas. He died on December 23, 1981, in San Antonio, Texas.

L. QUINCY MUMFORD (1954–1974)

On April 22, 1954, President Eisenhower nominated L. Quincy Mumford, director of the Cleveland Public Library and president-elect of the American Library Association, to be Librarian of Congress. Mumford, the first Librarian of Congress to graduate from a library school (B.S. degree in library science, Columbia University, 1929), was a popular choice. The Senate held hearings on July 26 and confirmed the nomination, without objection, on July 29. Librarian Mumford took the oath of office on September 1, 1954. It was administered by Associate Justice of the Supreme Court Harold H. Burton on the Library's 1782 Aiken Bible, the first complete Bible printed in English in the independent United States. Mumford retired on December 31, 1974. Lawrence Quincy Mumford was born on December 11, 1903, on a farm near Ayden in Pitt County, North Carolina. He died in Washington, D.C., on August 15, 1982.

DANIEL J. BOORSTIN (1975–1987)

Pres. Gerald R. Ford, on June 30, 1975, nominated author and historian Daniel J. Boorstin, senior historian and former director of the National Museum of History and Technology, Smithsonian Institution, to be Librarian of Congress. The nomination was supported by the Authors League of America but opposed by the American Library Association because the nominee "was not a library administrator." Hearings on the nomination were held on July 30 and 31 and September 10, 1975, and on September 26, 1975, the Senate confirmed the nomination without debate. Daniel J. Boorstin took the oath of office in the Library's Great Hall on November 12, 1975. Participants in the ceremony included the congressional leadership and Pres. Gerald R. Ford. The oath of office was administered by Speaker of the House of Representatives Carl Albert, on the Thompson Bible from the Library's Jefferson collection. Boorstin retired in 1987 in order to devote more time to writing and lecturing. He became Librarian of Congress Emeritus on August 4, 1987. Daniel J. Boorstin was born in Atlanta, Georgia, on October 1, 1914.

JAMES H. BILLINGTON (1987–   )

On April 17, 1987, Pres. Ronald Reagan nominated historian James H. Billington, director of the Woodrow Wilson International Center for Scholars at the Smithsonian Institution, to be the thirteenth Librarian of Congress. Hearings were held by the U.S. Senate on July 14, 1987; the American Library Association neither endorsed nor opposed the nomination. Billington was confirmed on July 24. He took the oath of office in the Library's Great Hall on September 14, 1987. Participants in the ceremony included the congressional leadership, Pres. Ronald Reagan, and Chief Justice William H. Rehnquist, who administered the oath on the Library's 1782 Aitken Bible. James H. Billington was born on June 1, 1929, in Bryn Mawr, Pennsylvania.

Notes

1. S. R. Ranganathan, "The Library of Congress Among National Libraries," *ALA Bulletin* 44 (October 1950): 356.

2. For a historical summary of the functions of the Library of Congress, *see* John Y. Cole, "For Congress & the Nation: The Dual Nature of the Library of Congress," *Quarterly Journal of the Library of Congress* 32 (April 1975): 119–38. Unless otherwise stated, dates and statistics are from John Y. Cole, *For Congress and the Nation: A Chronological History of the Library of Congress* (Washington, D.C.: Library of Congress, 1979).

3. Jefferson to Samuel H. Smith, September 21, 1814, Jefferson Papers, Library of Congress.

4. Ainsworth Rand Spofford, "The Government Library at Washington," *International Review* 5 (November 1878): 769.

5. "The Library of Congress. The Capitol and its Grounds." *Speech of the Hon. Justin S. Morrill of Vermont in the Senate of the United States, March 31, 1879* (Washington, 1879).

6. "The Library of Congress." *A Speech Delivered by the Hon. D. W. Voorhees of Indiana in the Senate of the United States, May 5, 1880* (Washington, 1880).

7. U.S. Congress, Joint Committee on the Library, *Condition of the Library of Congress,* March 3, 1897, 54th Cong., 2d sess., S. Rept. 1573, p. 142.

8. Herbert Putnam, "The Library of Congress as the National Library," *Library Journal* 30 (September 1905): c30.

9. John Y. Cole, "The Library of Congress and American Scholarship, 1865–1939," in *Libraries and Scholarly Communication in the United States: The Historical Dimension,*" ed. Phyllis Dain and John Y. Cole (N.Y.: Greenwood Press, 1990), pp. 45–61.

10. Herbert Putnam, "The Relation of the National Library to Historical Research in the United States," in *American Historical Association Annual Report for 1901* (Washington, D.C., 1902), p. 120.

11. U.S. Congress, *Congressional Record* 72 (June 9, 1930): 10347; U.S. Senate, Committee on the Library, *Purchase of Vollbehr Collection of Incunabula,* 71st Cong., 2d sess., 1930–31, S. Rept. 965, p 6.

12. U.S. Senate, Committee on the Library, *Legislative Drafting Bureau and Reference Division,* 62d Cong., 3d sess., 1913, S. Rept. 1271, p. 37.

13. Ibid., p. 29.

14. U.S. Library of Congress, *Report of the Librarian of Congress for the Fiscal Year Ending June 30, 1925.* (Washington, D.C.: Government Printing Office, 1925), p. 5.

15. James Truslow Adams, *The Epic of America* (N.Y.: Garden City Books, 1931), p. 325.

16. Luther H. Evans, "Library of Congress Records a New Era of World Progress," *The Sunday Star* (Washington, D.C.), December 2, 1945.

17. John Y. Cole, "The International Role of the Library of Congress. A Brief History," *Alexandria* 1 (December 1989): 43–51.

18. John Y. Cole, ed., *The Library of Congress in Perspective: A Volume Based on the Reports of the 1976 Librarian's Task Force and Advisory Groups* (N.Y., R. R. Bowker Company, 1978), pp. 85–147.

19. U.S. Library of Congress, "The Report of the Management and Planning Team to the Librarian of Congress," November 18, 1988. 259 p. (mimeographed).

20. James H. Billington, Statement Before the Subcommittee on Legislative Appropriations, Committee on Appropriations, U.S. House of Representatives, Fiscal 1993 Budget Request. Jan. 29, 1992.

21. Thomas Jefferson, Sixth Annual Message of the President of the United States, Dec. 2, 1806, in *Thomas Jefferson, Writings* (N.Y.: The Library of America, 1984), pp. 529–530.

Further Reading

Cole, John Y. "Of Copyright, Men, & a National Library," *Quarterly Journal of the Library Of Congress* 28: (April 1971): 114–36.

Cole, John Y. *For Congress and the Nation: A Chronological History of the Library of Congress.* Washington: Library of Congress, 1979.

Cole, John Y. "Studying the Library of Congress: Resources and Research Opportunities," *Libraries and Culture* 24 (Summer 1989): 357–66.

Goodrum, Charles A. and Helen W. Dalrymple. *Guide to the Library of Congress.* Washington: Library of Congress, 1988.

Goodrum, Charles A. and Helen W. Dalrymple. *The Library of Congress.* Boulder, Colo.: Westview Press, 1982.

Goodrum, Charles A. *Treasures of the Library of Congress.* Revised and expanded edition. N.Y.: H. N. Abrams, 1991.

Hilker, Helen-Anne. *Ten First Street, Southeast: Congress Builds a Library, 1886–1897.* Washington, Library of Congress, 1980.

Johnston, William Dawson. *History of the Library of Congress, 1800–1864.* Washington: Government Printing Office, 1904.

Lacy, Dan. "The Library of Congress: A Sesquicentenary Review," *Library Quarterly* 20 (1950): 157–179; 235–258.

Librarians of Congress, 1802–1974. Washington: Library of Congress, 1977.

McGuire, William. *Poetry's Catbird Seat: The Consultantship in Poetry in the English Language at the Library of Congress, 1937–1987.* Washington: Library of Congress, 1988.

Mearns, David C. *The Story Up To Now, The Library of Congress, 1800–1946.* Washington: Government Printing Office, 1947.

Melville, Annette. *Special Collections in the Library of Congress: A Selective Guide.* Washington: Library of Congress, 1980.

Nelson, Josephus, and Judith Farley. *Full Circle: Ninety Years of Service in the Main Reading Room.* Washington: Library of Congress, 1991.

Rosenberg, Jane. "Foundation for Service: the 1896 Hearings on the Library of Congress," *Journal of Library History* 21 (Winter 1986): 107–30.

Wilson, Douglas. "Thomas Jefferson and the Legacy of a National Library," *Wilson Library Bulletin* (February 1990): 37–41.

ISBN 0-16-041653-1